GED Math
in 10 Days!

The Most Effective GED
Math Crash Course

By

Reza Nazari

All inquiries should be addressed to:
info@effortlessMath.com
www.EffortlessMath.com

ISBN: 978-1-64612-253-0

Published by: **Effortless Math Education Inc.**

For Online Math Practice Visit www.EffortlessMath.com

Welcome to
GED Math Prep
2023

Thank you for choosing Effortless Math for your GED Math test preparation and congratulations on making the decision to take the GED test! It's a remarkable move you are taking, one that shouldn't be diminished in any capacity. That's why you need to use every tool possible to ensure you succeed on the test with the highest possible score, and this extensive study guide is one such tool.

If math has never been a strong subject for you, **don't worry**! This book will help you prepare for (and even ACE) the GED test's math section. As test day draws nearer, effective preparation becomes increasingly more important. Thankfully, you have this comprchcnsive study guide to help you get ready for the test. With this guide, you can feel confident that you will be more than ready for the GED Math test when the time comes.

First and foremost, it is important to note that this book is a study guide and not a textbook. It is best read from cover to cover. Every lesson of this "self-guided math book" was carefully developed to ensure that you are making the most effective use of your time while preparing for the test. This up-to-date guide reflects the 2023 test guidelines and will put you on the right track to hone your math skills, overcome exam anxiety, and boost your confidence, so that you can have your best to succeed on the GED Math test.

This study guide will:

☑ Explain the format of the GED Math test.

☑ Describe specific test-taking strategies that you can use on the test.

☑ Provide GED Math test-taking tips.

☑ Review all GED Math concepts and topics you will be tested on.

☑ Help you identify the areas in which you need to concentrate your study time.

☑ Offer exercises that help you develop the basic math skills you will learn in each section.

☑ Give **2 realistic and full-length practice tests** (featuring new question types) with detailed answers to help you measure your exam readiness and build confidence.

This resource contains everything you will ever need to succeed on the GED Math test. You'll get in-depth instructions on every math topic as well as tips and techniques on how to answer each question type. You'll also get plenty of practice questions to boost your test-taking confidence.

In addition, in the following pages you'll find:

➢ **How to Use This Book Effectively** – This section provides you with step-by-step instructions on how to get the most out of this comprehensive study guide.

➢ **How to study for the GED Math Test** – A six-step study program has been developed to help you make the best use of this book and prepare for your GED Math test. Here you'll find tips and strategies to guide your study program and help you understand GED Math and how to ace the test.

➢ **GED Math Review** – Learn everything you need to know about the GED Math test.

➢ **GED Math Test-Taking Strategies** – Learn how to effectively put these recommended test-taking techniques into use for improving your GED Math score.

➢ **Test Day Tips** – Review these tips to make sure you will do your best when the big day comes.

Effortless Math's GED Online Center

Effortless Math Online GED Center offers a complete study program, including the following:

✓ Step-by-step instructions on how to prepare for the GED Math test

✓ Numerous GED Math worksheets to help you measure your math skills

✓ Complete list of GED Math formulas

✓ Video lessons for all GED Math topics

✓ Full-length GED Math practice tests

✓ And much more…

No Registration Required.

Visit **EffortlessMath.com/GED** to find your online GED Math resources.

 www.EffortlessMath.com

How to Use This Book Effectively

Look no further when you need a study guide to improve your math skills to succeed on the math portion of the GED test. Each chapter of this comprehensive guide to the GED Math will provide you with the knowledge, tools, and understanding needed for every topic covered on the test.

It's imperative that you understand each topic before moving onto another one, as that's the way to guarantee your success. Each chapter provides you with examples and a step-by-step guide of every concept to better understand the content that will be on the test. To get the best possible results from this book:

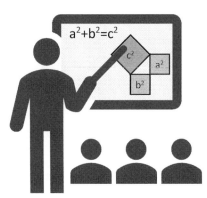

- ➢ **Begin studying long before your test date**. This provides you ample time to learn the different math concepts. The earlier you begin studying for the test, the sharper your skills will be. Do not procrastinate! Provide yourself with plenty of time to learn the concepts and feel comfortable that you understand them when your test date arrives.

- ➢ **Practice consistently**. Study GED Math concepts at least 1 to 2 hours a day in your 10-day study program. Remember, slow and steady wins the race, which can be applied to preparing for the GED Math test. Instead of cramming to tackle everything at once, be patient and learn the math topics in short bursts.

- ➢ Whenever you get a math problem wrong, **mark it off, and review it later** to make sure you understand the concept.

- ➢ Start each session by looking over the previous material.

- ➢ Once you've reviewed the book's lessons, **take a practice test at the back of the book** to gauge your level of readiness. Then, review your results. Read detailed answers and solutions for each question you missed.

- ➢ **Take another practice test** to get an idea of how ready you are to take the actual exam. Taking the practice tests will give you the confidence you need on test day. Simulate the GED testing environment by sitting in a quiet room free from distraction. Make sure to clock yourself with a timer.

How to Study for the GED Math Test

Studying for the GED Math test can be a really daunting and boring task. What's the best way to go about it? Is there a certain study method that works better than others? Well, studying for the GED Math can be done effectively. The following six-step program has been designed to make preparing for the GED Math test more efficient and less overwhelming.

Step **1** - Create a study plan
Step **2** - Choose your study resources
Step **3** - Review, Learn, Practice
Step **4** - Learn and practice test-taking strategies
Step **5** - Learn the GED Test format and take practice tests
Step **6** - Analyze your performance

STEP 1: Create a Study Plan

It's always easier to get things done when you have a plan. Creating a study plan for the GED Math test can help you to stay on track with your studies. It's important to sit down and prepare a study plan with what works with your life, work, and any other obligations you may have. Devote enough time each day to studying. It's also a great idea to break down each section of the exam into blocks and study one concept at a time.

It's important to understand that there is no "right" way to create a study plan. Your study plan will be personalized based on your specific needs and learning style.

Follow these guidelines to create an effective study plan for your GED Math test:

★ **Analyze your learning style and study habits** – Everyone has a different learning style. It is essential to embrace your individuality and the unique way you learn. Think about what works and what doesn't work for you. Do you prefer GED Math prep books or a combination of textbooks and video lessons? Does it work better for you if you study every night for thirty minutes or is it more effective to study in the morning before going to work?

★ **Evaluate your schedule** – Review your current schedule and find out how much time you can consistently devote to GED Math study.

★ **Develop a schedule** – Now it's time to add your study schedule to your calendar like any other obligation. Schedule time for study, practice, and review. Plan out which topic you will study on which day to ensure that you're devoting enough time to each concept. Develop a study plan that is mindful, realistic, and flexible.

★ **Stick to your schedule** – A study plan is only effective when it is followed consistently. You should try to develop a study plan that you can follow for the length of your study program.

★ **Evaluate your study plan and adjust as needed** – Sometimes you need to adjust your plan when you have new commitments. Check in with yourself regularly to make sure that you're not falling behind in your study plan. Remember, the most important thing is sticking to your plan. Your study plan is all about helping you be more productive. If you find that your study plan is not as effective as you want, don't get discouraged. It's okay to make changes as you figure out what works best for you.

STEP 2: Choose Your Study Resources

There are numerous textbooks and online resources available for the GED Math test, and it may not be clear where to begin. Don't worry! This study guide provides everything you need to fully prepare for your GED Math test. In addition to the book content, you can also use Effortless Math's online resources. (video lessons, worksheets, formulas, etc.)

Simply visit EffortlessMath.com/GED to find your online GED Math resources.

STEP 3: Review, Learn, Practice

This GED Math study guide breaks down each subject into specific skills or content areas. For instance, the percent concept is separated into different topics—percent calculation, percent increase and decrease, percent problems, etc. Use this book to help you go over all key math concepts and topics on the GED Math test.

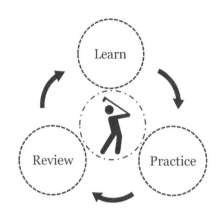

As you read each chapter, take notes or highlight the concepts you would like to go over again in the future. If you're unfamiliar with a topic or something is difficult for you, do additional research on it. For each math topic, plenty of instructions, step-by-step guides, and examples are provided to ensure you get a good grasp of the material. You can also find video lessons on the Effortless Math website for each GED Math concept.

Quickly review the topics you do understand to get a brush-up of the material. Be sure to do the practice questions provided at the end of every chapter to measure your understanding of the concepts.

STEP 4: Learn and Practice Test-taking Strategies

In the following sections, you will find important test-taking strategies and tips that can help you earn extra points. You'll learn how to think strategically and when to guess if you don't know the answer to a question. Using GED Math test-taking strategies and tips can help you raise your score and do well on the test. Apply test taking strategies on the practice tests to help you boost your confidence.

STEP 5: Learn the GED Test Format and Take Practice Tests

The *GED Test Review* section provides information about the structure of the GED test. Read this section to learn more about the GED test structure, different test sections, the number of questions in each section, and the section time limits. When you have a prior understanding of the test format and different types of GED Math questions, you'll feel more confident when you take the actual exam.

Once you have read through the instructions and lessons and feel like you are ready to go – take advantage of both of the full-length GED Math practice tests available in this study guide. Use the practice tests to sharpen your skills and build confidence.

The GED Math practice tests offered at the end of the book are formatted similarly to the actual GED Math test. When you take each practice test, try to simulate actual testing conditions. To take the practice tests, sit in a quiet space, time yourself, and work through as many of the questions as time allows. The practice tests are followed by detailed answer explanations to help you find your weak areas, learn from your mistakes, and raise your GED Math score.

STEP 6: Analyze Your Performance

After taking the practice tests, look over the answer keys and explanations to learn which questions you answered correctly and which you did not. Never be discouraged if you make a few mistakes. See them as a learning opportunity. This will highlight your strengths and weaknesses.

You can use the results to determine if you need additional practice or if you are ready to take the actual GED Math test.

Looking for more?

Visit EffortlessMath.com/GED to find hundreds of GED Math worksheets, video tutorials, practice tests, GED Math formulas, and much more.

Or scan this QR code.

No Registration Required.

GED Test Review

The General Educational Development Test, commonly known as the GED or high school equivalency degree, is a standardized test and is the only high school equivalency test recognized in all 50 USA states.

Currently, the GED is a computer-based test and is given at test centers all over the country. There are four subject area tests on GED:

➢ Reasoning through language arts

➢ Mathematical reasoning

➢ Social studies

➢ Science

The GED Test at a Glance:

Section	Overview	Testing time	Passing Score
Reasoning Through Language Arts	Reading and Writing Skills	150 minutes	145
Mathematical Reasoning	Quantitative Math and Algebra	115 minutes	145
Science	Life, earth and space, and physical sciences	90 minutes	145
Social Studies	Geography, civic, economics, and U.S. history	90 minutes	145

The GED Mathematical Reasoning test is a 115-minute, single-section test that covers basic mathematics topics, quantitative problem-solving and algebraic questions. There are two parts on the mathematical reasoning section. The first part contains 5 questions and calculators are not permitted. The second part contains 41 questions. A calculator is allowed in the second part. To learn more about how to use the calculator on your GED Math test, visit GED official website at: EffortlessMath.com/blog/ged-calculator

GED Math Question Types

The GED Math test has a variety of enhanced question types:

- Multiple-Choice – This is the most common type of question. Multiple-choice questions ask students to choose the one right answer out of four or five possible answer choices.

- Multiple-Select – This type of question is a little different than multiple-choice. Test takers will select all of the correct answer choices among a number of choices. Instead of having just one correct answer, there could be two or more correct answers.

- Fill-in-the-blank – Test takers type their answers in the box, either after a question or in the middle of a sentence. In math, the answer is often numerical but it can sometimes be a word or short phrase.

- Drag-and-Drop – Test takers will need to click and use a "draggable" option to move the answer over to the target region and question it relates to. Sometimes there might be two or more target regions.

- Matching – This question format requires test takers to check a box when data from a column matches the data in a row. True or False questions fall under this question type.

- Table-Entry – This type of question is used when there is a table of values of two columns. Certain cells in the table will have a box where the test taker types in a number to make the table correct.

How the GED is Scored?

Each GED area test is scored on a scale of 100-200 points. To pass the GED, you must earn at least 145 on each of the four subject tests, for a total of at least 580 points (out of a possible 800).

Each subject test should be passed individually. This means that you must get 145 on each section of the test. If you failed one subject test but did well enough on another to get a total score of 580, that's still not a passing score.

There are four possible scores that you can receive on the GED Test:

Not Passing: This indicates that your score is lower than 145 on any of the four tests. If you do not pass, you can reschedule up to two times a year to retake any or all subjects of the GED test.

Passing Score/High School Equivalency: This score indicates that your score is between 145-164. Remember that points on one subject of the test do not carry over to the other subjects.

College Ready: This indicates that your score is between 165-175, demonstrating career and college readiness. A College Ready score shows that you may not need placement testing or remediation before beginning a college degree program.

College Ready + Credit: This indicates that your score is 175 or higher. This shows that you've already mastered some skills that would be taught in college courses. Depending on a school's policy, this can translate to some college credits—saving you time and money during your college education.

There are approximately 46 questions on GED Mathematical Reasoning. Similar to other subject areas, you will need a minimum score of 145 to pass the Mathematical Reasoning Test. There are 49 raw score points on the GED math test. These raw points correspond with correct answers. Most questions have one answer; therefore, they only have one point. There is more than one point for questions that have more than one answer. You'll get a raw score out of the 49 possible points. This will then be converted into your scaled score out of 200. You will need to get about 32 out of 49 raw points to pass the Mathematical Reasoning section.

GED Math Test-Taking Strategies

Here are some test-taking strategies that you can use to maximize your performance and results on the GED Math test.

#1 : USE THIS APPROACH TO ANSWER EVERY GED MATH QUESTION

- Review the question to identify keywords and important information.
- Translate the keywords into math operations so you can solve the problem.
- Review the answer choices. What are the differences between answer choices?
- Draw or label a diagram if needed.
- Try to find patterns.
- Find the right method to answer the question. Use straightforward math, plug in numbers, or test the answer choices (backsolving).
- Double-check your work

#2 : USE EDUCATED GUESSING

This approach is applicable to the problems you understand to some degree but cannot solve using straightforward math. In such cases, try to filter out as many answer choices as possible before picking an answer. In cases where you don't have a clue about what a certain problem entails, don't waste any time trying to eliminate answer choices. Just choose one randomly before moving onto the next question.

As you can ascertain, direct solutions are the most optimal approach. Carefully read through the question, determine what the solution is using the math you have learned before, then coordinate the answer with one of the choices available to you. Are you stumped? Make your best guess, then move on.

Don't leave any fields empty! Even if you're unable to work out a problem, strive to answer it. Take a guess if you have to. You will not lose points by getting an answer wrong, though you may gain a point by getting it correct!

#**3** : BALLPARK

A ballpark answer is a rough approximation. When we become overwhelmed by calculations and figures, we end up making silly mistakes. A decimal that is moved by one unit can change an answer from right to wrong, regardless of the number of steps that you went through to get it. That's where ballparking can play a big part.

If you think you know what the correct answer may be (even if it's just a ballpark answer), you'll usually have the ability to eliminate a couple of choices. While answer choices are usually based on the average student error and/or values that are closely tied, you will still be able to weed out choices that are way far afield. Try to find answers that aren't in the proverbial ballpark when you're looking for a wrong answer on a multiple-choice question. This is an optimal approach to eliminating answers to a problem.

#**4** : BACKSOLVING

A majority of questions on the GED Math test will be in multiple-choice format. Many test-takers prefer multiple-choice questions, as at least the answer is right there. You'll typically have four answers to pick from. You simply need to figure out which one is correct. Usually, the best way to go about doing so is "backsolving."

As mentioned earlier, direct solutions are the most optimal approach to answering a question. Carefully read through a problem, calculate a solution, then correspond the answer with one of the choices displayed in front of you. If you can't calculate a solution, your next best approach involves "backsolving."

When backsolving a problem, contrast one of your answer options against the problem you are asked, then see which of them is most relevant. More often than not, answer choices are listed in ascending or descending order. In such cases, try out the choices B or C. If it's not correct, you can go either down or up from there.

#5 : Plugging In Numbers

"Plugging in numbers" is a strategy that can be applied to a wide range of different math problems on the GED Math test. This approach is typically used to simplify a challenging question so that it is more understandable. By using the strategy carefully, you can find the answer without too much trouble.

The concept is fairly straightforward–replace unknown variables in a problem with certain values. When selecting a number, consider the following:

- Choose a number that's basic (just not too basic). Generally, you should avoid choosing 1 (or even 0). A decent choice is 2.

- Try not to choose a number that is displayed in the problem.

- Make sure you keep your numbers different if you need to choose at least two of them.

- More often than not, choosing numbers merely lets you filter out some of your answer choices. As such, don't just go with the first choice that gives you the right answer.

- If several answers seem correct, then you'll need to choose another value and try again. This time, though, you'll just need to check choices that haven't been eliminated yet.

- If your question contains fractions, then a potential right answer may involve either an LCD (least common denominator) or an LCD multiple.

- 100 is the number you should choose when you are dealing with problems involving percentages.

GED Math – Test Day Tips

After practicing and reviewing all the math concepts you've been taught, and taking some GED mathematics practice tests, you'll be prepared for test day. Consider the following tips to be extra-ready come test time.

Before Your Test

What to do the night before:

- **Relax!** One day before your test, study lightly or skip studying altogether. You shouldn't attempt to learn something new, either. There are plenty of reasons why studying the evening before a big test can work against you. Put it this way–a marathoner wouldn't go out for a sprint before the day of a big race. Mental marathoners–such as yourself–should not study for any more than one hour 24 hours before a GED test. That's because your brain requires some rest to be at its best. The night before your exam, spend some time with family or friends, or read a book.

- **Avoid bright screens** - You'll have to get some good shuteye the night before your test. Bright screens (such as the ones coming from your laptop, TV, or mobile device) should be avoided altogether. Staring at such a screen will keep your brain up, making it hard to drift asleep at a reasonable hour.

- **Make sure your dinner is healthy** - The meal that you have for dinner should be nutritious. Be sure to drink plenty of water as well. Load up on your complex carbohydrates, much like a marathon runner would do. Pasta, rice, and potatoes are ideal options here, as are vegetables and protein sources.

- **Get your bag ready for test day** - The night prior to your test, pack your bag with your stationery, admissions pass, ID, and any other gear that you need. Keep the bag right by your front door.

- **Make plans to reach the testing site** - Before going to sleep, ensure that you understand precisely how you will arrive at the site of the test. If parking is something you'll have to find first, plan for it. If you're dependent on public transit, then review the schedule. You should also make sure that the train/bus/subway/streetcar you use will be running. Find out about road closures as well. If a parent or friend is accompanying you, ensure that they understand what steps they have to take as well.

The Day of the Test

■ **Get up reasonably early, but not too early.**

■ **Have breakfast** - Breakfast improves your concentration, memory, and mood. As such, make sure the breakfast that you eat in the morning is healthy. The last thing you want to be is distracted by a grumbling tummy. If it's not your own stomach making those noises, another test taker close to you might be instead. Prevent discomfort or embarrassment by consuming a healthy breakfast. Bring a snack with you if you think you'll need it.

■ **Follow your daily routine** - Do you watch Good Morning America each morning while getting ready for the day? Don't break your usual habits on the day of the test. Likewise, if coffee isn't something you drink in the morning, then don't take up the habit hours before your test. Routine consistency lets you concentrate on the main objective–doing the best you can on your test.

■ **Wear layers** - Dress yourself up in comfortable layers. You should be ready for any kind of internal temperature. If it gets too warm during the test, take a layer off.

■ **Get there on time** - The last thing you want to do is get to the test site late. Rather, you should be there 45 minutes prior to the start of the test. Upon your arrival, try not to hang out with anybody who is nervous. Any anxious energy they exhibit shouldn't influence you.

■ **Leave the books at home** - No books should be brought to the test site. If you start developing anxiety before the test, books could encourage you to do some last-minute studying, which will only hinder you. Keep the books far away–better yet, leave them at home.

- **Make your voice heard** - If something is off, speak to a proctor. If medical attention is needed or if you'll require anything, consult the proctor prior to the start of the test. Any doubts you have should be clarified. You should be entering the test site with a state of mind that is completely clear.

- **Have faith in yourself** - When you feel confident, you will be able to perform at your best. When you are waiting for the test to begin, envision yourself receiving an outstanding result. Try to see yourself as someone who knows all the answers, no matter what the questions are. A lot of athletes tend to use this technique—particularly before a big competition. Your expectations will be reflected by your performance.

During your test

- **Be calm and breathe deeply** - You need to relax before the test, and some deep breathing will go a long way to help you do that. Be confident and calm. You got this. Everybody feels a little stressed out just before an evaluation of any kind is set to begin. Learn some effective breathing exercises. Spend a minute meditating before the test starts. Filter out any negative thoughts you have. Exhibit confidence when having such thoughts.

- **Concentrate on the test** - Refrain from comparing yourself to anyone else. You shouldn't be distracted by the people near you or random noise. Concentrate exclusively on the test. If you find yourself irritated by surrounding noises, earplugs can be used to block sounds off close to you. Don't forget—the test is going to last several hours if you're taking more than one subject of the test. Some of that time will be dedicated to brief sections. Concentrate on the specific section you are working on during a particular moment. Do not let your mind wander off to upcoming or previous sections.

- **Skip challenging questions** - Optimize your time when taking the test. Lingering on a single question for too long will work against you. If you don't know what the answer is to a certain question, use your best guess, and mark the question so you can review it later on. There is no need to spend time attempting to solve something you aren't sure about. That time would be better served handling the questions you can actually answer well. You will not be penalized for getting the wrong answer on a test like this.

- **Try to answer each question individually** - Focus only on the question you are working on. Use one of the test-taking strategies to solve the problem. If you aren't able to come up with an answer, don't get frustrated. Simply skip that question, then move onto the next one.

- **Don't forget to breathe!** Whenever you notice your mind wandering, your stress levels boosting, or frustration brewing, take a thirty-second break. Shut your eyes, drop your pencil, breathe deeply, and let your shoulders relax. You will end up being more productive when you allow yourself to relax for a moment.

- **Review your answer.** If you still have time at the end of the test, don't waste it. Go back and check over your answers. It is worth going through the test from start to finish to ensure that you didn't make a sloppy mistake somewhere.

- **Optimize your breaks** - When break time comes, use the restroom, have a snack, and reactivate your energy for the subsequent section. Doing some stretches can help stimulate your blood flow.

After your test

- **Take it easy** - You will need to set some time aside to relax and decompress once the test has concluded. There is no need to stress yourself out about what you could've said, or what you may have done wrong. At this point, there's nothing you can do about it. Your energy and time would be better spent on something that will bring you happiness for the remainder of your day.

■ **Redoing the test** - Did you pass the test? Congratulations! Your hard work paid off! Passing this test means that you are now as knowledgeable as somebody who has graduated high school.

If you have failed your test, though, don't worry! The test can be retaken. In such cases, you will need to follow the retake policy established by your state. You also need to re-register to take the exam again.

Contents

DAY 4

Exponents and Variables 43

DAY 5

Expressions and Variables 57

DAY 6

Equations and Inequalities 69

DAY 7

Lines and Slope 81

Fractions and Mixed Numbers

Math topics that you'll learn in this chapter:

1. Simplifying Fractions
2. Adding and Subtracting Fractions
3. Multiplying and Dividing Fractions
4. Adding Mixed Numbers
5. Subtracting Mixed Numbers
6. Multiplying Mixed Numbers
7. Dividing Mixed Numbers

Simplifying Fractions

☆ A fraction contains two numbers separated by a bar between them. The bottom number, called the denominator, is the total number of equally divided portions in one whole. The top number, called the numerator, is how many portions you have. And the bar represents the operation of division.

☆ Simplifying a fraction means reducing it to the lowest terms. To simplify a fraction, evenly divide both the top and bottom of the fraction by $2, 3, 5, 7$, etc.

☆ Continue until you can't go any further.

Examples:

Example 1. Simplify $\frac{16}{24}$

Solution: To simplify $\frac{16}{24}$, find a number that both 16 and 24 are divisible by. Both are divisible by 8. Then: $\frac{16}{24} = \frac{16 \div 8}{24 \div 8} = \frac{2}{3}$

Example 2. Simplify $\frac{36}{96}$

Solution: To simplify $\frac{36}{96}$, find a number that both 36 and 96 are divisible by. Both are divisible by 6 and 12. Then: $\frac{36}{96} = \frac{36 \div 6}{96 \div 6} = \frac{6}{16}$, 6 and 16 are divisible by 2, then: $\frac{6}{16} = \frac{3}{8}$ or $\frac{36}{96} = \frac{36 \div 12}{96 \div 12} = \frac{3}{8}$

Example 3. Simplify $\frac{43}{129}$

Solution: To simplify $\frac{43}{129}$, find a number that both 43 and 129 are divisible by. Both are divisible by 43, then: $\frac{43}{129} = \frac{43 \div 43}{129 \div 43} = \frac{1}{3}$

Adding and Subtracting Fractions

☆ For "like" fractions (fractions with the same denominator), add or subtract the numerators (top numbers) and write the answer over the common denominator (bottom numbers).

☆ Adding and Subtracting fractions with the same denominator:

$$\frac{a}{b} + \frac{c}{b} = \frac{a+c}{b}, \frac{a}{b} - \frac{c}{b} = \frac{a-c}{b}$$

☆ Find equivalent fractions with the same denominator before you can add or subtract fractions with different denominators.

☆ Adding and Subtracting fractions with different denominators:

$$\frac{a}{b} + \frac{c}{d} = \frac{ad+bc}{bd}, \frac{a}{b} - \frac{c}{d} = \frac{ad-bc}{bd}$$

Examples:

Example 1. Find the sum. $\frac{3}{4} + \frac{2}{3} =$

Solution: These two fractions are "unlike" fractions. (they have different denominators). Use this formula: $\frac{a}{b} + \frac{c}{d} = \frac{ad+cb}{bd}$

Then: $\frac{3}{4} + \frac{2}{3} = \frac{(3)(3)+(4)(2)}{4 \times 3} = \frac{9+8}{12} = \frac{17}{12}$

Example 2. Find the difference. $\frac{4}{7} - \frac{2}{5} =$

Solution: For "unlike" fractions, find equivalent fractions with the same denominator before you can add or subtract fractions with different denominators. Use this formula: $\frac{a}{b} - \frac{c}{d} = \frac{ad-bc}{bd}$

$\frac{4}{7} - \frac{2}{5} = \frac{(4)(5)-(2)(7)}{7 \times 5} = \frac{20-14}{35} = \frac{6}{35}$

Multiplying and Dividing Fractions

☆ **Multiplying fractions:** multiply the top numbers and multiply the bottom numbers. Simplify if necessary. $\frac{a}{b} \times \frac{c}{d} = \frac{a \times c}{b \times d}$

☆ **Dividing fractions:** Keep, Change, Flip

☆ Keep the first fraction, change the division sign to multiplication, and flip the numerator and denominator of the second fraction. Then, solve!

$$\frac{a}{b} \div \frac{c}{d} = \frac{a}{b} \times \frac{d}{c} = \frac{a \times d}{b \times c}$$

Examples:

Example 1. Multiply. $\frac{3}{4} \times \frac{2}{5} =$

Solution: Multiply the top numbers and multiply the bottom numbers.
$\frac{3}{4} \times \frac{2}{5} = \frac{3 \times 2}{4 \times 5} = \frac{6}{20}$, now, simplify: $\frac{6}{20} = \frac{6 \div 2}{20 \div 2} = \frac{3}{10}$

Example 2. Solve. $\frac{2}{3} \div \frac{3}{7} =$

Solution: Keep the first fraction, change the division sign to multiplication, and flip the numerator and denominator of the second fraction.
Then: $\frac{2}{3} \div \frac{3}{7} = \frac{2}{3} \times \frac{7}{3} = \frac{2 \times 7}{3 \times 3} = \frac{14}{9}$

Example 3. Calculate. $\frac{6}{5} \times \frac{2}{3} =$

Solution: Multiply the top numbers and multiply the bottom numbers.
$\frac{6}{5} \times \frac{2}{3} = \frac{6 \times 2}{5 \times 3} = \frac{12}{15}$, simplify: $\frac{12}{15} = \frac{12 \div 3}{15 \div 3} = \frac{4}{5}$

Example 4. Solve. $\frac{4}{5} \div \frac{3}{8} =$

Solution: Keep the first fraction, change the division sign to multiplication, and flip the numerator and denominator of the second fraction.
Then: $\frac{4}{5} \div \frac{3}{8} = \frac{4}{5} \times \frac{8}{3} = \frac{4 \times 8}{5 \times 3} = \frac{32}{15}$

Adding Mixed Numbers

Use the following steps for adding mixed numbers:

✰ Add whole numbers of the mixed numbers.

✰ Add the fractions of the mixed numbers.

✰ Find the Least Common Denominator (LCD) if necessary.

✰ Add whole numbers and fractions.

✰ Write your answer in lowest terms.

Examples:

Example 1. Add mixed numbers. $3\frac{2}{3} + 1\frac{2}{5} =$

Solution: Let's rewriting our equation with parts separated,
$3\frac{2}{3} + 1\frac{2}{5} = 3 + \frac{2}{3} + 1 + \frac{2}{5}$. Now, add whole number parts: $3 + 1 = 4$. Add the fraction parts $\frac{2}{3} + \frac{2}{5}$. Rewrite to solve with the equivalent fractions. $\frac{2}{3} + \frac{2}{5} = \frac{10}{15} + \frac{6}{15} = \frac{16}{15}$. The answer is an improper fraction (numerator is bigger than denominator). Convert the improper fraction into a mixed number: $\frac{16}{15} = 1\frac{1}{15}$. Now, combine the whole and fraction parts: $4 + 1\frac{1}{15} = 5\frac{1}{15}$.

Example 2. Find the sum. $2\frac{1}{2} + 1\frac{3}{5} =$

Solution: Rewriting our equation with parts separated, $2 + \frac{1}{2} + 1 + \frac{3}{5}$. Add the whole number parts: $2 + 1 = 3$. Add the fraction parts: $\frac{1}{2} + \frac{3}{5} = \frac{5}{10} + \frac{6}{10} = \frac{11}{10}$. Convert the improper fraction into a mixed number: $\frac{11}{10} = 1\frac{1}{10}$. Now, combine the whole and fraction parts: $3 + 1\frac{1}{10} = 4\frac{1}{10}$.

Subtracting Mixed Numbers

Use these steps for subtracting mixed numbers.

☆ Convert mixed numbers into improper fractions. $a\frac{c}{b} = \frac{ab+c}{b}$

☆ Find equivalent fractions with the same denominator for unlike fractions. (fractions with different denominators)

☆ Subtract the second fraction from the first one. $\frac{a}{b} - \frac{c}{d} = \frac{ad-bc}{bd}$

☆ Write your answer in lowest terms.

☆ If the answer is an improper fraction, convert it into a mixed number.

Examples:

Example 1. Subtract. $2\frac{1}{5} - 1\frac{2}{3} =$

Solution: Convert mixed numbers into fractions:

$2\frac{1}{5} = \frac{2\times5+1}{5} = \frac{11}{5}$ and $1\frac{2}{3} = \frac{1\times3+2}{3} = \frac{5}{3}$

These two fractions are "unlike" fractions. (they have different denominators).

Find equivalent fractions with the same denominator. Use this formula:

$$\frac{a}{b} - \frac{c}{d} = \frac{ad - bc}{bd}$$

$\frac{11}{5} - \frac{5}{3} = \frac{(11)(3)-(5)(5)}{5\times 3} = \frac{33-25}{15} = \frac{8}{15}$

Example 2. Find the difference. $2\frac{3}{7} - 1\frac{4}{5} =$

Solution: Convert mixed numbers into fractions:

$2\frac{3}{7} = \frac{2\times7+3}{7} = \frac{17}{7}$ and $1\frac{4}{5} = \frac{1\times5+4}{5} = \frac{9}{5}$

Then: $2\frac{3}{7} - 1\frac{4}{5} = \frac{17}{7} - \frac{9}{5} = \frac{(17)(5)-(9)(7)}{7\times 5} = \frac{85-63}{35} = \frac{22}{35}$

Multiplying Mixed Numbers

Use the following steps for multiplying mixed numbers:

☆ Convert the mixed numbers into fractions. $a\frac{c}{b} = a + \frac{c}{b} = \frac{ab+c}{b}$

☆ Multiply fractions. $\frac{a}{b} \times \frac{c}{d} = \frac{a \times c}{b \times d}$

☆ Write your answer in lowest terms.

☆ If the answer is an improper fraction (numerator is bigger than denominator), convert it into a mixed number.

Examples:

Example 1. Multiply. $3\frac{1}{3} \times 2\frac{3}{5} =$

Solution: Convert mixed numbers into fractions,
$3\frac{1}{3} = \frac{3\times3+1}{3} = \frac{10}{3}$ and $2\frac{3}{5} = \frac{2\times5+3}{5} = \frac{13}{5}$. Apply the fractions rule for multiplication:
$\frac{10}{3} \times \frac{13}{5} = \frac{10 \times 13}{3 \times 5} = \frac{130}{15} = \frac{130 \div 5}{15 \div 5} = \frac{26}{3}$
The answer is an improper fraction. Convert it into a mixed number. $\frac{26}{3} = 8\frac{2}{3}$

Example 2. Multiply. $2\frac{3}{4} \times 4\frac{3}{7} =$

Solution: Converting mixed numbers into fractions, $2\frac{3}{4} \times 4\frac{3}{7} = \frac{11}{4} \times \frac{31}{7}$
Apply the fractions rule for multiplication: $\frac{11}{4} \times \frac{31}{7} = \frac{11\times31}{4\times7} = \frac{341}{28} = 12\frac{5}{28}$

Example 3. Find the product. $4\frac{3}{5} \times 3\frac{4}{6} =$

Solution: Convert mixed numbers to fractions: $4\frac{3}{5} = \frac{23}{5}$ and $3\frac{4}{6} = \frac{22}{6} = \frac{22\div2}{6\div2} = \frac{11}{3}$.

Multiply two fractions:

$\frac{23}{5} \times \frac{11}{3} = \frac{23\times11}{5\times3} = \frac{253}{15} = 16\frac{13}{15}$

Dividing Mixed Numbers

Use the following steps for dividing mixed numbers:

☆ Convert the mixed numbers into fractions. $a\frac{c}{b} = a + \frac{c}{b} = \frac{ab+c}{b}$

☆ Divide fractions: Keep, Change, Flip: Keep the first fraction, change the division sign to multiplication, and flip the numerator and denominator of the second fraction. Then, solve! $\frac{a}{b} \div \frac{c}{d} = \frac{a}{b} \times \frac{d}{c} = \frac{a \times d}{b \times c}$

☆ Write your answer in lowest terms.

☆ If the answer is an improper fraction (numerator is bigger than denominator), convert it into a mixed number.

Examples:

Example 1. Solve. $2\frac{2}{3} \div 1\frac{1}{2} =$

Solution: Convert mixed numbers into fractions:
$2\frac{2}{3} = \frac{2 \times 3 + 2}{3} = \frac{8}{3}$ and $1\frac{1}{2} = \frac{1 \times 2 + 1}{2} = \frac{3}{2}$
Keep, Change, Flip: $\frac{8}{3} \div \frac{3}{2} = \frac{8}{3} \times \frac{2}{3} = \frac{8 \times 2}{3 \times 3} = \frac{16}{9}$. The answer is an improper fraction.
Convert it into a mixed number: $\frac{16}{9} = 1\frac{7}{9}$

Example 2. Solve. $4\frac{2}{3} \div 1\frac{3}{5} =$

Solution: Convert mixed numbers to fractions, then solve:
$4\frac{2}{3} \div 1\frac{3}{5} = \frac{14}{3} \div \frac{8}{5} = \frac{14}{3} \times \frac{5}{8} = \frac{70}{24} = 2\frac{11}{12}$

Example 3. Solve. $3\frac{2}{5} \div 2\frac{1}{3} =$

Solution: Converting mixed numbers to fractions: $3\frac{2}{5} \div 2\frac{1}{3} = \frac{17}{5} \div \frac{7}{3}$
Keep, Change, Flip: $\frac{17}{5} \div \frac{7}{3} = \frac{17}{5} \times \frac{3}{7} = \frac{17 \times 3}{5 \times 7} = \frac{51}{35} = 1\frac{16}{35}$

Day 1: Practices

✎ Simplify each fraction.

1) $\frac{2}{8} =$

2) $\frac{5}{15} =$

3) $\frac{12}{36} =$

4) $\frac{65}{120} =$

✎ Find the sum or difference.

5) $\frac{3}{10} + \frac{2}{10} =$

6) $\frac{4}{5} + \frac{1}{10} =$

7) $\frac{3}{4} + \frac{6}{20} =$

8) $\frac{4}{9} - \frac{1}{9} =$

9) $\frac{3}{8} - \frac{1}{6} =$

10) $\frac{9}{21} - \frac{2}{7} =$

✎ Find the products or quotients.

11) $\frac{3}{4} \div \frac{9}{12} =$

12) $\frac{7}{10} \div \frac{21}{20} =$

13) $\frac{12}{21} \div \frac{3}{7} =$

14) $\frac{12}{5} \times \frac{10}{24} =$

15) $\frac{33}{36} \times \frac{3}{4} =$

16) $\frac{7}{9} \times \frac{1}{3} =$

✎ Find the sum.

17) $3\frac{1}{2} + 1\frac{3}{4} =$

18) $4\frac{1}{8} + 2\frac{7}{8} =$

19) $4\frac{1}{2} + 2\frac{3}{8} =$

20) $1\frac{2}{21} + 4\frac{4}{7} =$

21) $6\frac{3}{5} + 1\frac{2}{3} =$

22) $2\frac{3}{11} + 3\frac{1}{2} =$

✎ Find the difference.

23) $6\frac{2}{3} - 4\frac{1}{3} =$

24) $5\frac{2}{5} - 3\frac{1}{5} =$

25) $8\frac{1}{2} - 3\frac{1}{4} =$

26) $7\frac{2}{3} - 2\frac{1}{6} =$

✍ Find the products.

27) $1\frac{2}{3} \times 2\frac{3}{4} =$

28) $1\frac{1}{6} \times 1\frac{3}{5} =$

29) $4\frac{1}{2} \times 1\frac{2}{3} =$

30) $2\frac{1}{2} \times 4\frac{4}{5} =$

31) $2\frac{1}{5} \times 4\frac{1}{2} =$

32) $1\frac{1}{9} \times 2\frac{3}{5} =$

✍ Solve.

33) $3\frac{1}{3} \div 1\frac{2}{3} =$

34) $4\frac{2}{3} \div 2\frac{1}{2} =$

35) $6\frac{1}{5} \div 2\frac{1}{3} =$

36) $2\frac{2}{3} \div 1\frac{4}{9} =$

37) $4\frac{1}{6} \div 2\frac{1}{8} =$

38) $3\frac{2}{5} \div 1\frac{5}{4} =$

39) A pizza cut into 6 parts. David and his sister Sara ordered two pizzas. David ate $\frac{1}{3}$ of his pizza and Eva ate $\frac{1}{2}$ of her pizza. What part of the two pizzas was left?

40) Jake is preparing to run a marathon. He runs $9\frac{1}{3}$ miles on Saturday and two times that many on Monday and Wednesday. Jake wants to run a total of 50 miles this week. How many more miles does he need to run?

41) Last week 21,000 fans attended a football match. This week four times as many bought tickets, but one third of them cancelled their tickets. How many are attending this week?

42) In a bag of small balls $\frac{1}{2}$ are black, $\frac{1}{4}$ are white, $\frac{1}{8}$ are red and the remaining 16 blue. How many balls are white?

Day 1: Answers

1) $\frac{2}{8} = \frac{2 \div 2}{8 \div 2} = \frac{1}{4}$

2) $\frac{5}{15} = \frac{5 \div 5}{15 \div 5} = \frac{1}{3}$

3) $\frac{12}{36} = \frac{12 \div 12}{36 \div 12} = \frac{1}{3}$

4) $\frac{65}{120} = \frac{65 \div 5}{120 \div 5} = \frac{13}{24}$

5) $\frac{3}{10} + \frac{2}{10} = \frac{3+2}{10} = \frac{5}{10} = \frac{5 \div 5}{10 \div 5} = \frac{1}{2}$

6) $\frac{4}{5} + \frac{1}{10} = \frac{4 \times 2}{5 \times 2} + \frac{1}{10} = \frac{8}{10} + \frac{1}{10} = \frac{8+1}{10} = \frac{9}{10}$

7) $\frac{3}{4} + \frac{6}{20} = \frac{3 \times 5}{4 \times 5} + \frac{6}{20} = \frac{15}{20} + \frac{6}{20} = \frac{21}{20}$

8) $\frac{4}{9} - \frac{1}{9} = \frac{4-1}{9} = \frac{3}{9} = \frac{3 \div 3}{9 \div 3} = \frac{1}{3}$

9) $\frac{3}{8} - \frac{1}{6} = \frac{3 \times 6}{8 \times 6} - \frac{1 \times 8}{6 \times 8} = \frac{18}{48} - \frac{8}{48} = \frac{18-8}{48} = \frac{10}{48} = \frac{10 \div 2}{48 \div 2} = \frac{5}{24}$

10) $\frac{9}{21} - \frac{2}{7} = \frac{9}{21} - \frac{2 \times 3}{7 \times 3} = \frac{9}{21} - \frac{6}{21} = \frac{9-6}{21} = \frac{3}{21} = \frac{3 \div 3}{21 \div 3} = \frac{1}{7}$

11) $\frac{3}{4} \div \frac{9}{12} = \frac{3}{4} \times \frac{12}{9} = \frac{36}{36} = 1$

12) $\frac{7}{10} \div \frac{21}{20} = \frac{7}{10} \times \frac{20}{21} = \frac{140}{210} = \frac{140 \div 70}{210 \div 70} = \frac{2}{3}$

13) $\frac{12}{21} \div \frac{3}{7} = \frac{12 \div 3}{21 \div 3} \times \frac{7}{3} = \frac{4}{7} \times \frac{7}{3} = \frac{28}{21} = \frac{28 \div 7}{21 \div 7} = \frac{4}{3}$

14) $\frac{12}{5} \times \frac{10}{24} = \frac{120}{120} = 1$

15) $\frac{33}{36} \times \frac{3}{4} = \frac{33 \div 3}{36 \div 3} \times \frac{3}{4} = \frac{11}{12} \times \frac{3}{4} = \frac{33 \div 3}{48 \div 3} = \frac{11}{16}$

16) $\frac{7}{9} \times \frac{1}{3} = \frac{7}{27}$

17) $3\frac{1}{2} + 1\frac{3}{4} \rightarrow 3 + \frac{1}{2} + 1 + \frac{3}{4} \rightarrow 3 + 1 = 4, \ \frac{1}{2} + \frac{3}{4} = \frac{1 \times 2}{2 \times 2} + \frac{3}{4} = \frac{2}{4} + \frac{3}{4} = \frac{2+3}{4} = \rightarrow$
$\frac{5}{4} = 1\frac{1}{4}, \ 4 + 1\frac{1}{4} = 5\frac{1}{4}$

18) $4\frac{1}{8} + 2\frac{7}{8} \rightarrow 4 + \frac{1}{8} + 2 + \frac{7}{8} \rightarrow 4 + 2 = 6, \ \frac{1}{8} + \frac{7}{8} = \frac{1+7}{8} = \frac{8}{8} = 1 \rightarrow 6 + 1 = 7$

19) $4\frac{1}{2} + 2\frac{3}{8} \rightarrow 4 + \frac{1}{2} + 2 + \frac{3}{8} \rightarrow 4 + 2 = 6, \ \frac{1}{2} + \frac{3}{8} = \frac{1 \times 4}{2 \times 4} + \frac{3}{8} = \frac{4}{8} + \frac{3}{8} = \frac{4+3}{8} = \frac{7}{8} \rightarrow$
$6 + \frac{7}{8} = 6\frac{7}{8}$

20) $1\frac{2}{21} + 4\frac{4}{7} \rightarrow 1 + \frac{2}{21} + 4 + \frac{4}{7} \rightarrow 1 + 4 = 5, \ \frac{2}{21} + \frac{4}{7} = \frac{2}{21} + \frac{4 \times 3}{7 \times 3} + = \frac{2}{21} + \frac{12}{21} = \frac{2+12}{21} = \frac{14}{21} =$
$\frac{14 \div 7}{21 \div 7} = \frac{2}{3}$
$\rightarrow 5 + \frac{2}{3} = 5\frac{2}{3}$

21) $6\frac{3}{5} + 1\frac{2}{3} \rightarrow 6 + \frac{3}{5} + 1 + \frac{2}{3} \rightarrow 6 + 1 = 7, \ \frac{3}{5} + \frac{2}{3} = \frac{3 \times 3}{5 \times 3} + \frac{2 \times 5}{3 \times 5} = \frac{9}{15} + \frac{10}{15} = \frac{9+10}{15} = \frac{19}{15} = 1\frac{4}{15} \rightarrow$

$$7 + 1\frac{4}{15} = 8\frac{4}{15}$$

22) $2\frac{3}{11} + 3\frac{1}{2} \rightarrow 2 + \frac{3}{11} + 3 + \frac{1}{2} \rightarrow 2 + 3 = 5, \quad \frac{3}{11} + \frac{1}{2} = \frac{3 \times 2}{11 \times 2} + \frac{1 \times 11}{2 \times 11} = \frac{6}{22} + \frac{11}{22} = \frac{6+11}{22} = \frac{17}{22}$

$\rightarrow 5 + \frac{17}{22} = 5\frac{17}{22}$

23) $6\frac{2}{3} - 4\frac{1}{3} \rightarrow 6 + \frac{2}{3} - 4 - \frac{1}{3} \rightarrow 6 - 4 = 2, \quad \frac{2}{3} - \frac{1}{3} = \rightarrow \frac{2-1}{3} = \frac{1}{3} \rightarrow 2 + \frac{1}{3} = 2\frac{1}{3}$

24) $5\frac{2}{5} - 3\frac{1}{5} \rightarrow 5 + \frac{2}{5} - 3 - \frac{1}{5} \rightarrow 5 - 3 = 2, \quad \frac{2}{5} - \frac{1}{5} = \frac{1}{5} \rightarrow 2 + \frac{1}{5} = 2\frac{1}{5}$

25) $8\frac{1}{2} - 3\frac{1}{4} \rightarrow 8 + \frac{1}{2} - 3 - \frac{1}{4} \rightarrow 8 - 3 = 5, \quad \frac{1}{2} - \frac{1}{4} = \frac{1 \times 2}{2 \times 2} - \frac{1}{4} = \frac{1}{4} \rightarrow 5 + \frac{1}{4} = 5\frac{1}{4}$

26) $7\frac{2}{3} - 2\frac{1}{6} \rightarrow 7 + \frac{2}{3} - 2 - \frac{1}{6} \rightarrow 7 - 2 = 5, \quad \frac{2}{3} - \frac{1}{6} = \frac{2 \times 2}{3 \times 2} - \frac{1}{6} = \frac{3 \div 3}{6 \div 3} = \frac{1}{2} \rightarrow 5 + \frac{1}{2} = 5\frac{1}{2}$

27) $1\frac{2}{3} \times 2\frac{3}{4} \rightarrow 1\frac{2}{3} = \frac{1 \times 3 + 2}{3} = \frac{5}{3}, 2\frac{3}{4} = \frac{2 \times 4 + 3}{4} = \frac{11}{4} \rightarrow \frac{5}{3} \times \frac{11}{4} = \frac{5 \times 11}{3 \times 4} = \frac{55}{12} = 4\frac{7}{12}$

28) $1\frac{1}{6} \times 1\frac{3}{5} \rightarrow 1\frac{1}{6} = \frac{1 \times 6 + 1}{6} = \frac{7}{6}, 1\frac{3}{5} = \frac{1 \times 5 + 3}{5} = \frac{8}{5} \rightarrow \frac{7}{6} \times \frac{8}{5} = \frac{7 \times 8}{6 \times 5} = \frac{56}{30} = \frac{56 \div 2}{30 \div 2} = \frac{28}{15} = 1\frac{13}{15}$

29) $4\frac{1}{2} \times 1\frac{2}{3} \rightarrow 4\frac{1}{2} = \frac{4 \times 2 + 1}{2} = \frac{9}{2}, 1\frac{2}{3} = \frac{1 \times 3 + 2}{3} = \frac{5}{3} \rightarrow \frac{9}{2} \times \frac{5}{3} = \frac{9 \times 5}{2 \times 3} = \frac{45}{6} = \frac{45 \div 3}{6 \div 3} = \frac{15}{2} = 7\frac{1}{2}$

30) $2\frac{1}{2} \times 4\frac{4}{5} \rightarrow 2\frac{1}{2} = \frac{2 \times 2 + 1}{2} = \frac{5}{2}, 4\frac{4}{5} = \frac{4 \times 5 + 4}{5} = \frac{24}{5} \rightarrow \frac{5}{2} \times \frac{24}{5} = \frac{5 \times 24}{2 \times 5} = \frac{120}{10} = 12$

31) $2\frac{1}{5} \times 4\frac{1}{2} \rightarrow 2\frac{1}{5} = \frac{2 \times 5 + 1}{5} = \frac{11}{5}, 4\frac{1}{2} = \frac{4 \times 2 + 1}{2} = \frac{9}{2} \rightarrow \frac{11}{5} \times \frac{9}{2} = \frac{11 \times 9}{5 \times 2} = \frac{99}{10} = 9\frac{9}{10}$

32) $1\frac{1}{9} \times 2\frac{3}{5} \rightarrow 1\frac{1}{9} = \frac{1 \times 9 + 1}{9} = \frac{10}{9}, 2\frac{3}{5} = \frac{2 \times 5 + 3}{5} = \frac{13}{5} \rightarrow \frac{10}{9} \times \frac{13}{5} = \frac{10 \times 13}{9 \times 5} = \frac{130}{45} = \frac{130 \div 5}{45 \div 5} \rightarrow$

$\frac{26}{9} = 2\frac{8}{9}$

33) $3\frac{1}{3} \div 1\frac{2}{3} \rightarrow 3\frac{1}{3} = \frac{3 \times 3 + 1}{3} = \frac{10}{3}, 1\frac{2}{3} = \frac{1 \times 3 + 2}{3} = \frac{5}{3} \rightarrow \frac{10}{3} \div \frac{5}{3} = \frac{10}{3} \times \frac{3}{5} = \frac{30}{15} = 2$

34) $4\frac{2}{3} \div 2\frac{1}{2} \rightarrow 4\frac{2}{3} = \frac{4 \times 3 + 2}{3} = \frac{14}{3}, 2\frac{1}{2} = \frac{2 \times 2 + 1}{2} = \frac{5}{2} \rightarrow \frac{14}{3} \div \frac{5}{2} = \frac{14}{3} \times \frac{2}{5} = \frac{28}{15} = 1\frac{13}{15}$

35) $6\frac{1}{5} \div 2\frac{1}{3} \rightarrow 6\frac{1}{5} = \frac{6 \times 5 + 1}{5} = \frac{31}{5}, 2\frac{1}{3} = \frac{2 \times 3 + 1}{3} = \frac{7}{3} \rightarrow \frac{31}{5} \div \frac{7}{3} = \frac{31}{5} \times \frac{3}{7} = \frac{93}{35} = 2\frac{23}{35}$

36) $2\frac{2}{3} \div 1\frac{4}{9} \rightarrow 2\frac{2}{3} = \frac{2 \times 3 + 2}{3} = \frac{8}{3}, 1\frac{4}{9} = \frac{1 \times 9 + 4}{9} = \frac{13}{9} \rightarrow \frac{8}{3} \div \frac{13}{9} = \frac{8}{3} \times \frac{9}{13} = \frac{72 \div 3}{39 \div 3} = \frac{24}{13} = 1\frac{11}{13}$

37) $4\frac{1}{6} \div 2\frac{1}{8} \rightarrow 4\frac{1}{6} = \frac{4 \times 6 + 1}{6} = \frac{25}{6}, 2\frac{1}{8} = \frac{2 \times 8 + 1}{8} = \frac{17}{8} \rightarrow \frac{25}{6} \div \frac{17}{8} = \frac{25}{6} \times \frac{8}{17} = \frac{200 \div 2}{102 \div 2} \rightarrow$

$\frac{100}{51} = 1\frac{49}{51}$

38) $3\frac{2}{5} \div 1\frac{5}{4} \rightarrow 3\frac{2}{5} = \frac{3 \times 5 + 2}{5} = \frac{17}{5}, 1\frac{5}{4} = \frac{1 \times 4 + 5}{4} = \frac{9}{4} \rightarrow \frac{17}{5} \div \frac{9}{4} = \frac{17}{5} \times \frac{4}{9} = \frac{68}{45} = 1\frac{23}{45}$

39) David ate $\frac{1}{3}$ of 6 parts of his pizza $\rightarrow \frac{1}{3} \times 6 = \frac{6 \div 3}{3 \div 3} = 2 \rightarrow$ It means 2 parts out of 6 parts and left 4 parts. Sara ate $\frac{1}{2}$ of 6 parts of her pizza:

$\rightarrow \frac{1}{2} \times 6 = \frac{6 \div 2}{2 \div 2} = 3 \rightarrow$ It means 3 parts out of 6 parts and left 3 parts. Therefore, they ate $(2 + 3)$ parts out of $(6 + 6)$ parts of their pizza and left $(4 + 3)$ parts out of $(6 + 6)$ parts of their pizza that equals to: $\frac{7}{12}$

40) Jake run $9\frac{1}{3}$ miles on Saturday and $2 \times \left(9\frac{1}{3}\right)$ miles on Monday and Wednesday. Jake wants to run a total of 50 miles this week. Therefore, $9\frac{1}{3} + 2 \times \left(9\frac{1}{3}\right)$ should be subtracted from 50:

$50 - \left(9\frac{1}{3} + \left(2 \times 9\frac{1}{3}\right)\right) = 50 - \left(\frac{9 \times 3 + 1}{3} + \left(2 \times \frac{9 \times 3 + 1}{3}\right)\right) = 50 - \left(\frac{28}{3} + \frac{56}{3}\right) = 50 - \left(\frac{28 + 56}{3}\right) = 50 - \left(\frac{84}{3}\right) = 50 - (28) = 22$ miles.

41) Four times of 21,000 is 84,000. One third of them cancelled their tickets. One third of 84,000 Equals 28,000. $(\frac{1}{3} \times 84,000 = 28,000)$.

84,000 – 28,000 = 56,000 fans are attending this week.

42) Let x be the total number of balls. Then: $\frac{1}{2}x + \frac{1}{4}x + \frac{1}{8}x + 16 = x$

$\left(\frac{1}{2} + \frac{1}{4} + \frac{1}{8}\right)x + 16 = x \rightarrow \left(\frac{1 \times 4}{2 \times 4} + \frac{1 \times 2}{4 \times 2} + \frac{1}{8}\right)x + 16 = x \rightarrow$

$\left(\frac{4}{8} + \frac{2}{8} + \frac{1}{8}\right)x + 16 = x \rightarrow \left(\frac{7}{8}\right)x + 16 = x \rightarrow 16 = x - \frac{7}{8}x \rightarrow 16 = \frac{1}{8}x$

$\rightarrow$ Multiply both sides by 8: $16 \times 8 = \frac{1}{8}x \times 8 \rightarrow 128 = x$

x is the total number of balls. Therefore, number of white balls is:

$\frac{1}{4}x = \frac{1}{4} \times 128 = 32$

DAY 2 Decimals and Integers

Math topics that you'll learn in this chapter:

1. Comparing Decimals
2. Rounding Decimals
3. Adding and Subtracting Decimals
4. Multiplying and Dividing Decimals
5. Adding and subtracting Integers
6. Multiplying and Dividing Integers
7. Order of Operations
8. Integers and Absolute Value

15

Comparing Decimals

☆ A decimal is a fraction written in a special form. For example, instead of writing $\frac{1}{2}$ you can write: 0.5

☆ A Decimal Number contains a Decimal Point. It separates the whole number part from the fractional part of a decimal number.

☆ Let's review decimal place values: Example: 45.3861

4: tens	5: ones	3: tenths
8: hundredths	6: thousandths	1: tens thousandths

☆ To compare two decimals, compare each digit of two decimals in the same place value. Start from left. Compare hundreds, tens, ones, tenth, hundredth, etc.

☆ To compare numbers, use these symbols:

Equal to =	Less than <	Greater than >
Less than or equal ≤	Greater than or equal ≥	

Examples:

Example 1. Compare 0.05 and 0.50.

Solution: 0.50 is greater than 0.05, because the tenth place of 0.50 is 5, but the tenth place of 0.05 is zero. Then: $0.05 < 0.50$

Example 2. Compare 0.0512 and 0.181.

Solution: 0.181 is greater than 0.0512, because the tenth place of 0.181 is 1, but the tenth place of 0.0512 is zero. Then: $0.0512 < 0.181$

Rounding Decimals

✩ We can round decimals to a certain accuracy or number of decimal places. This is used to make calculations easier to do and results easier to understand when exact values are not too important.

✩ First, you'll need to remember your place values: For example: 12.4869

1: tens   2: ones   4: tenths

8: hundredths   6: thousandths   9: tens thousandths

✩ To round a decimal, first find the place value you'll round to.

✩ Find the digit to the right of the place value you're rounding to. If it is 5 or bigger, add 1 to the place value you're rounding to and remove all digits on its right side. If the digit to the right of the place value is less than 5, keep the place value and remove all digits on the right.

Examples:

Example 1. Round 3.2568 to the thousandth-place value.

Solution: First, look at the next place value to the right, (tens thousandths). It's 8 and it is greater than 5. Thus add 1 to the digit in the thousandth place. The thousandth place is 6.→ 6 + 1 = 7, then, the answer is 3.257.

Example 2. Round 2.3628 to the nearest hundredth.

Solution: First, look at the digit to the right of hundredth (thousandths place value). It's 2 and it is less than 5, thus remove all the digits to the right of hundredth place. Then, the answer is 2.36.

Adding and Subtracting Decimals

☆ Line up the decimal numbers.

☆ Add zeros to have the same number of digits for both numbers if necessary.

☆ Remember your place values: For example: 73.5196

     7: tens   3: ones   5: tenths

     1: hundredths   9: thousandths   6: tens thousandths

☆ Add or subtract using column addition or subtraction.

Examples:

Example 1. Add. $2.6 + 3.25 =$

Solution: First, line up the numbers: $\begin{array}{r} 2.6 \\ +3.25 \\ \hline \end{array}$ →Add a zero to have the same number of digits for both numbers. $\begin{array}{r} 2.60 \\ +3.25 \\ \hline \end{array}$ →Start with the hundredths place: $0 + 5 = 5$, $\begin{array}{r} 2.60 \\ +3.25 \\ \hline 5 \end{array}$ →Continue with tenths place: $6 + 2 = 8$, $\begin{array}{r} 2.60 \\ +3.25 \\ \hline .85 \end{array}$ →Add the ones place: $2 + 3 = 5$, $\begin{array}{r} 2.60 \\ +3.25 \\ \hline 5.85 \end{array}$. The answer is 5.85.

Example 2. Find the difference. $4.26 - 3.12 =$

Solution: First, line up the numbers: $\begin{array}{r} 4.26 \\ -3.12 \\ \hline \end{array}$ →Start with the hundredths place: $6 - 2 = 4$, $\begin{array}{r} 4.26 \\ -3.12 \\ \hline 4 \end{array}$ → Continue with tenths place. $2 - 1 = 1$, $\begin{array}{r} 4.26 \\ -3.12 \\ \hline .14 \end{array}$ →Subtract the ones place. $4 - 3 = 1$, $\begin{array}{r} 4.26 \\ -3.12 \\ \hline 1.14 \end{array}$

Multiplying and Dividing Decimals

For multiplying decimals:

⭐ Ignore the decimal point and set up and multiply the numbers as you do with whole numbers.

⭐ Count the total number of decimal places in both of the factors.

⭐ Place the decimal point in the product.

For dividing decimals:

⭐ If the divisor is not a whole number, move the decimal point to the right to make it a whole number. Do the same for the dividend.

⭐ Divide similar to whole numbers.

Examples:

Example 1. Find the product. $0.53 \times 0.32 =$

Solution: Set up and multiply the numbers as you do with whole numbers. Line up the numbers: $\begin{array}{r} 53 \\ \times 32 \end{array}$ →Start with the ones place then continue with other digits $\rightarrow \begin{array}{r} 53 \\ \times 32 \\ \hline 1,696 \end{array}$. Count the total number of decimal places in both of the factors. There are four decimals digits. (two for each factor 0.53 and 0.32) Then:

$0.53 \times 0.32 = 0.1696$

Example 2. Find the quotient. $1.50 \div 0.5 =$

Solution: The divisor is not a whole number. Multiply it by 10 to get 5:
$\rightarrow 0.5 \times 10 = 5$

Do the same for the dividend to get 15. $\rightarrow 1.50 \times 10 = 15$

Now, divide $15 \div 5 = 3$. The answer is 3.

Adding and Subtracting Integers

✰ Integers include zero, counting numbers, and the negative of the counting numbers$\{..., -3, -2, -1, 0, 1, 2, 3, ...\}$

✰ Add a positive integer by moving to the right on the number line. (you will get a bigger number)

✰ Add a negative integer by moving to the left on the number line. (you will get a smaller number)

✰ Subtract an integer by adding its opposite.

Number line

Examples:

Example 1. Solve. $(-3) - (-5) =$

Solution: Keep the first number and convert the sign of the second number to its opposite. (change subtraction into addition. Then: $(-3) + 5 = 2$

Example 2. Solve. $5 + (2 - 8) =$

Solution: First, subtract the numbers in brackets, $2 - 8 = -6$
Then: $5 + (-6) =\rightarrow$change addition into subtraction: $5 - 6 = -1$

Example 3. Solve. $(8 - 15) + 14 =$

Solution: First, subtract the numbers in brackets, $8 - 15 = -7$
Then: $-7 + 14 =\rightarrow -7 + 14 = 7$

Example 4. Solve. $18 + (-5 - 17) =$

Solution: First, subtract the numbers in brackets, $-5 - 17 = -22$
Then: $18 + (-22) =\rightarrow$change addition into subtraction: $18 - 22 = -4$

Multiplying and Dividing Integers

Use the following rules for multiplying and dividing integers:

☆ (negative) × (negative) = positive

☆ (negative) ÷ (negative) = positive

☆ (negative) × (positive) = negative

☆ (negative) ÷ (positive) = negative

☆ (positive) × (positive) = positive

☆ (positive) ÷ (negative) = negative

Examples:

Example 1. Solve. $5 \times (-2) =$

Solution: Use this rule: (positive) × (negative) = negative.
Then: $(5) \times (-2) = -10$

Example 2. Solve. $(-2) + (-30 \div 6) =$

Solution: First, divide -30 by 6, the numbers in brackets, use this rule:
(negative) ÷ (positive) = negative. Then: $-30 \div 6 = -5$
$(-2) + (-30 \div 6) = (-2) + (-5) = -2 - 5 = -7$

Example 3. Solve. $(13 - 16) \times (-3) =$

Solution: First, subtract the numbers in brackets,
$13 - 16 = -3 \rightarrow (-3) \times (-3) =$
Now use this rule: (negative) × (negative) = positive $\rightarrow (-3) \times (-3) = 9$

Example 4. Solve. $(18 - 3) \div (-5) =$

Solution: First, subtract the numbers in brackets,
$18 - 3 = 15 \rightarrow (15) \div (-5) =$
Now use this rule: (positive) ÷ (negative) = negative $\rightarrow (15) \div (-5) = -3$

Order of Operations

☆ In Mathematics, "operations" are addition, subtraction, multiplication, division, exponentiation (written as b^n) and grouping.

☆ When there is more than one math operation in an expression, use PEMDAS: (to memorize this rule, remember the phrase "Please Excuse My Dear Aunt Sally".)

❖ Parentheses

❖ Exponents

❖ Multiplication and Division (from left to right)

❖ Addition and Subtraction (from left to right)

Examples:

Example 1. Calculate. $(3 + 5) \div (8 \div 4) =$

Solution: First, simplify inside parentheses:
$(3 + 5) \div (8 \div 4) = (8) \div (8 \div 4) = (8) \div (2)$. Then: $(8) \div (2) = 4$

Example 2. Solve. $(4 \times 3) - (14 - 3) =$

Solution: First, calculate within parentheses: $(4 \times 3) - (14 - 3) = (12) - (11)$, Then: $(12) - (11) = 1$

Example 3. Calculate. $-3[(6 \times 5) \div (5 \times 3)] =$

Solution: First, calculate within parentheses:
$-3[(6 \times 5) \div (5 \times 3)] = -3[(30) \div (5 \times 3)] = -3[(30) \div (15)] = -3[2]$
Multiply -3 and 2. Then: $-3[2] = -6$

Example 4. Solve. $(32 \div 4) + (-25 + 5) =$

Solution: First, calculate within parentheses:
$(32 \div 4) + (-25 + 5) = (8) + (-20)$. Then: $(8) - (20) = -12$

Integers and Absolute Value

☆ The absolute value of a number is its distance from zero, in either direction, on the number line. For example, the distance of 9 and -9 from zero on number line is 9.

☆ The absolute value of an integer is the numerical value without its sign. (negative or positive)

☆ The vertical bar is used for absolute value as in $|x|$.

☆ The absolute value of a number is never negative; because it only shows, "how far the number is from zero".

Examples:

Example 1. Calculate. $|15 - 3| \times 6 =$

Solution: First, solve $|15 - 3| \rightarrow |15 - 3| = |12|$, the absolute value of 12 is 12, $|12| = 12$. Then: $12 \times 6 = 72$

Example 2. Solve. $|-35| \times |6 - 10| =$

Solution: First, find $|-35| \rightarrow$ the absolute value of -35 is 35. Then: $|-35| = 35$, $|-35| \times |6 - 10| =$
Now, calculate $|6 - 10| \rightarrow |6 - 10| = |-4|$, the absolute value of -4 is 4. $|-4| = 4$
Then: $35 \times 4 = 140$

Example 3. Solve. $|12 - 6| \times \frac{|-4 \times 5|}{3} =$

Solution: First, calculate $|12 - 6| \rightarrow |12 - 6| = |6|$, the absolute value of 6 is 6, $|6| = 6$. Then: $6 \times \frac{|-4 \times 5|}{3} =$
Now calculate $|-4 \times 5| \rightarrow |-4 \times 5| = |-20|$, the absolute value of -20 is 20, $|-20| = 20$. Then: $6 \times \frac{20}{3} = \frac{6 \times 20}{3} = \frac{120}{3} = 40$

Day 2: Practices

✍ Compare. Use >, =, and <

1) $0.3 \square 0.2$
2) $0.98 \square 0.71$

3) $5.01 \square 5.0100$
4) $0.427 \square 0.435$

✍ Round each decimal to the nearest whole number.

5) 4.9
6) 6.3

7) 75.66
8) 93.03

✍ Find the sum or difference.

9) $2.5 + 11.1 =$
10) $12.83 + 14.11 =$

11) $13.8 - 9.2 =$
12) $43.55 - 21.32 =$

✍ Find the product or quotient.

13) $5.1 \times 0.2 =$
14) $0.35 \times 1.2 =$

15) $2.1 \div 0.3$
16) $25.5 \div 0.5$

✍ Find each sum or difference.

17) $-6 + 17 =$
18) $12 - 21 =$
19) $31 - (-4) =$

20) $(7 + 5) + (8 - 3) =$
21) $(2 - 3) - (15 - 11) =$
22) $(-8 - 7) - (-6 - 2) =$

✍ Solve.

23) $2 \times (-4) =$

24) $(-5) \times (-3) =$

25) $(-15) \div 5 =$

26) $(-4) \times (-5) \times (-2) =$

27) $(-6 + 36) \div (-2) =$

28) $(-25 + 5) \times (-5 - 3) =$

✍ Evaluate each expression.

29) $5 - (2 \times 3) =$

30) $(6 \times 5) - 8 =$

31) $(-5 \times 3) + 4 =$

32) $(-35 \div 5) - (12 + 2) =$

33) $4 \times [(2 \times 3) \div (-3 + 1)] =$

34) $35 \div [(6 - 1) \times (7 - 8)] =$

✍ Find the answers.

35) $|-3| + |7 - 9| =$

36) $|8 - 10| + |6 - 7| =$

37) $|-6 + 10| - |-9 - 3| =$

38) $3 + |2 - 1| + |3 - 12| =$

39) $-8 - |3 - 6| + |2 + 3| =$

40) $|-6| \times |-5.4| =$

41) $|3 \times (-4)| \times \frac{8}{3} =$

42) $|(-2) \times (-2)| \times \frac{1}{4} =$

43) $|-8| + |(-8) \times 2| =$

44) $|(-3) \times (-5)| \times |(-3) \times (-4)| =$

✍ Find the answers.

45) Round 4.2873 to the thousandth-place value

46) $[6 \times (-16) + 8] - (-4) + [4 \times 5] \div 2 =$

Day 2: Answers

1) $0.3 > 0.2$

2) $0.98 > 0.71$

3) $5.01 = 5.0100$

4) $0.427 < 0.435$

5) $4.9 \approx 5$

6) $6.3 \approx 6$

7) $75.66 \approx 76$

8) $93.03 \approx 93$

9) $\begin{array}{r}2.5\\ +11.1\\ \hline\end{array} \to 5 + 1 = 6 \to \begin{array}{r}2.5\\ +11.1\\ \hline .6\end{array} \to 2 + 1 = 3 \to \begin{array}{r}2.5\\ +11.1\\ \hline 3.6\end{array} \to 0 + 1 = 1 \to \begin{array}{r}2.5\\ +11.1\\ \hline 13.6\end{array}$

10) $\begin{array}{r}12.83\\ +14.11\\ \hline\end{array} \to 3 + 1 = 4 \to \begin{array}{r}12.83\\ +14.11\\ \hline 4\end{array} \to 8 + 1 = 9 \to \begin{array}{r}12.83\\ +14.11\\ \hline .94\end{array} \to 2 + 4 = 6 \to \begin{array}{r}12.83\\ +14.11\\ \hline 6.94\end{array} \to 1 + 1 = 2 \to \begin{array}{r}12.83\\ +14.11\\ \hline 26.94\end{array}$

11) $\begin{array}{r}13.8\\ -9.2\\ \hline\end{array} \to 8 - 2 = 6 \to \begin{array}{r}13.8\\ -9.2\\ \hline .6\end{array} \to 13 - 9 = 4 \to \begin{array}{r}13.8\\ -9.2\\ \hline 4.6\end{array}$

12) $\begin{array}{r}43.55\\ -21.32\\ \hline\end{array} \to 5 - 2 = 3 \to \begin{array}{r}43.55\\ -21.32\\ \hline 3\end{array} \to 5 - 3 = 2 \to \begin{array}{r}43.55\\ -21.32\\ \hline 23\end{array} \to 3 - 1 = 2 \to \begin{array}{r}43.55\\ -21.32\\ \hline 2.23\end{array} \to 4 - 2 = 2 \to \begin{array}{r}43.55\\ -21.32\\ \hline 22.23\end{array}$

13) $5.1 \times 0.2 \to \begin{array}{r}51\\ \times 2\\ \hline 102\end{array} \to 5.1 \times 0.2 = 1.02$

14) $0.35 \times 1.2 \to \begin{array}{r}35\\ \times 12\\ \hline 70\\ +350\\ \hline 420\end{array} \to 0.35 \times 1.2 = 0.420$

15) $2.1 \div 0.3 \to \dfrac{2.1 \times 10}{0.3 \times 10} = \dfrac{21}{3} = 7$

16) $25.5 \div 0.5 \to \dfrac{25.50 \times 10}{0.5 \times 10} = \dfrac{255}{5} = 51$

17) $-6 + 17 = 17 - 6 = 11$

18) $12 - 21 = -9$

19) $31 - (-4) = 31 + 4 = 35$

20) $(7 + 5) + (8 - 3) = 12 + 5 = 17$

21) $(2 - 3) - (15 - 11) = (-1) - (4) = -1 - 4 = -5$

22) $(-8 - 7) - (-6 - 2) = (-15) - (-8) = -15 + 8 = -7$

23) Use this rule: (positive) × (negative) = negative → $2 \times (-4) = -8$

24) Use this rule: (negative) × (negative) = positive → $(-5) \times (-3) = 15$

25) Use this rule: (negative) ÷ (positive) = negative → $(-15) \div 5 = -3$

26) Use these rules: [(negative) × (negative) = positive] and [(positive) × (negative) = negative]→ $(-4) \times (-5) \times (-2) = (20) \times (-2) = -40$

27) Use this rule: (positive)÷ (negative) = negative→
$(-6 + 36) \div (-2) = (30) \div (-2) = -15$

28) Use this rule: (negative) × (negative) = positive→
$(-25 + 5) \times (-5 - 3) = (-20) \times (-8) = -160$

29) $5 - (2 \times 3) = 5 - 6 = -1$

30) $(6 \times 5) - 8 = 30 - 8 = 22$

31) Use this rule: (negative) × (positive) = negative → $(-5 \times 3) + 4 = -15 + 4 = -11$

32) Use this rule: (negative) ÷ (positive) = negative →
$(-35 \div 5) - (12 + 2) = -7 - 14 = -21$

33) Use these rules: [(positive) × (negative) = negative] and [(positive) ÷ (negative) = negative]→ $4 \times [(2 \times 3) \div (-3 + 1)] = 4 \times [6 \div (-2)] = 4 \times (-3) = -12$

34) Use these rules: [(positive) × (negative) = negative] and [(positive) ÷ (negative) = negative]→ $35 \div [(6 - 1) \times (7 - 8)] = 35 \div [5 \times (-1)] = 35 \div (-5) = -7$

35) $|-3| + |7 - 9| = 3 + |-2| = 3 + 2 = 5$

36) $|8 - 10| + |6 - 7| = |-2| + |-1| = 2 + 1 = 3$

37) $|-6 + 10| - |-9 - 3| = |4| - |-12| = 4 - (12) = 4 - 12 = -8$

38) $3 + |2 - 1| + |3 - 12| = 3 + |1| + |-9| = 3 + 1 + (9) = 3 + 1 + 9 = 13$

39) $-8 - |3 - 6| + |2 + 3| = -8 - |-3| + |5| = -8 - (3) + 5 = -8 - 3 + 5 = -11 + 5 = -6$

40) $|-6| \times |-5.4| = 6 \times 5.4 = 32.4$

41) $|3 \times (-4)| \times \frac{8}{3} = |-12| \times \frac{8}{3} = 12 \times \frac{8}{3} = \frac{12 \times 8}{3} = 32$

42) $|(-2) \times (-2)| \times \frac{1}{4} = |4| \times \frac{1}{4} = 4 \times \frac{1}{4} = 1$

43) $|-8| + |(-8) \times 2| = 8 + |-16| = 8 + 16 = 24$

44) $|(-3) \times (-5)| \times |(-3) \times (-4)| = |15| \times |12| = 15 \times 12 = 180$

45) $4.2873 \approx 4.287$

46) $[6 \times (-16) + 8] - (-4) + [4 \times 5] \div 2 = [(-96) + 8] - (-4) + [4 \times 5] \div 2 = (-88) - (-4) + (20) \div 2 = (-88) - (-4) + 10 = (-88) + 4 + (10) = -84 + 10 = -74$

DAY 3

Ratios, Proportions and Percent

Math topics that you'll learn in this chapter:

1. Simplifying Ratios
2. Proportional Ratios
3. Similarity and Ratios
4. Percent Problems
5. Percent of increase and Decrease
6. Discount, Tax and Tip
7. Simple Interest

29

Simplifying Ratios

☆ Ratios are used to make comparisons between two numbers.

☆ Ratios can be written as a fraction, using the word "to", or with a colon. Example: $\frac{3}{4}$ or "3 to 4" or 3:4

☆ You can calculate equivalent ratios by multiplying or dividing both sides of the ratio by the same number.

Examples:

Example 1. Simplify. $10:2 =$

Solution: Both numbers 10 and 2 are divisible by $2 \Rightarrow 10 \div 2 = 5, 2 \div 2 = 1$.
Then: $10:2 = 5:1$

Example 2. Simplify. $\frac{6}{33} =$

Solution: Both numbers 6 and 33 are divisible by $3 \Rightarrow 33 \div 3 = 11, 6 \div 3 = 2$.
Then: $\frac{6}{33} = \frac{2}{11}$

Example 3. There are 30 students in a class and 12 are girls. Find the ratio of girls to boys in that class.

Solution: Subtract 12 from 30 to find the number of boys in the class.
$30 - 12 = 18$. There are 18 boys in the class. So, the ratio of girls to boys is $12:18$.
Now, simplify this ratio. Both 18 and 12 are divisible by 6.
Then: $18 \div 6 = 3$, and $12 \div 6 = 2$. In the simplest form, this ratio is $2:3$

Example 4. A recipe calls for butter and sugar in the ratio $2:3$. If you're using 6 cups of butter, how many cups of sugar should you use?

Solution: Since you use 6 cups of butter, or 3 times as much, you need to multiply the amount of sugar by 3. Then: $3 \times 3 = 9$. So, you need to use 9 cups of sugar. You can solve this using equivalent fractions: $\frac{2}{3} = \frac{6}{9}$

Proportional Ratios

★ Two ratios are proportional if they represent the same relationship.

★ A proportion means that two ratios are equal. It can be written in two ways: $\frac{a}{b} = \frac{c}{d}$ $a : b = c : d$

★ The proportion $\frac{a}{b} = \frac{c}{d}$ can be written as: $a \times d = c \times b$

Examples:

Example 1. Solve this proportion for x. $\frac{3}{4} = \frac{9}{x}$

Solution: Use cross multiplication: $\frac{3}{4} = \frac{9}{x} \Rightarrow 3 \times x = 4 \times 9 \Rightarrow 3x = 36$

Divide both sides by 3 to find x: $x = \frac{36}{3} \Rightarrow x = 12$

Example 2. If a box contains red and blue balls in ratio of $4 : 7$ red to blue, how many red balls are there if 49 blue balls are in the box?

Solution: Write a proportion and solve. $\frac{4}{7} = \frac{x}{49}$

Use cross multiplication: $4 \times 49 = 7 \times x \Rightarrow 196 = 7x$

Divide to find x: $x = \frac{196}{7} \Rightarrow x = 28$. There are 28 red balls in the box.

Example 3. Solve this proportion for x. $\frac{5}{8} = \frac{20}{x}$

Solution: Use cross multiplication: $\frac{5}{8} = \frac{20}{x} \Rightarrow 5 \times x = 8 \times 20 \Rightarrow 5x = 160$

Divide to find x: $x = \frac{160}{5} \Rightarrow x = 32$

Example 4. Solve this proportion for x. $\frac{7}{9} = \frac{21}{x}$

Solution: Use cross multiplication: $\frac{7}{9} = \frac{21}{x} \Rightarrow 7 \times x = 9 \times 21 \Rightarrow 7x = 189$

Divide to find x: $x = \frac{189}{7} \Rightarrow x = 27$

Similarity and Ratios

☆ Two figures are similar if they have the same shape.

☆ Two or more figures are similar if the corresponding angles are equal, and the corresponding sides are in proportion.

Examples:

Example 1. The following triangles are similar. What is the value of the unknown side?

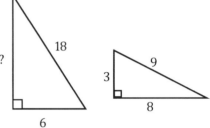

Solution: Find the corresponding sides and write a proportion.
$\frac{9}{18} = \frac{8}{x}$. Now, use the cross product to solve for x:
$\frac{9}{18} = \frac{8}{x} \rightarrow 9 \times x = 18 \times 8 \rightarrow 9x = 144$. Divide both sides by 9. Then: $9x = 144 \rightarrow x = \frac{144}{9} \rightarrow x = 16$

The missing side is 16.

Example 2. Two rectangles are similar. The first is 4 feet wide and 12 feet long. The second is 8 feet wide. What is the length of the second rectangle?

Solution: Let's put x for the length of the second rectangle. Since two rectangles are similar, their corresponding sides are in proportion. Write a proportion and solve for the missing number.
$\frac{4}{8} = \frac{12}{x} \rightarrow 4x = 8 \times 12 \rightarrow 4x = 96 \rightarrow x = \frac{96}{4} = 24$
The length of the second rectangle is 24 feet.

Percent Problems

★ Percent is a ratio of a number and 100. It always has the same denominator, 100. The percent symbol is "%".

★ Percent means "per 100". So, 20% is $\frac{20}{100}$.

★ In each percent problem, we are looking for the base, or the part or the percent.

★ Use these equations to find each missing section in a percent problem:

  ❖ Base = Part ÷ Percent

  ❖ Part = Percent × Base

  ❖ Percent = Part ÷ Base

Examples:

Example 1. What is 30% of 60?

Solution: In this problem, we have the percent (30%) and the base (60) and we are looking for the "part". Use this formula: *Part = Percent × Base*.
Then: $Part = 30\% \times 60 = \frac{30}{100} \times 60 = 0.30 \times 60 = 18$. The answer: 30% of 60 is 18.

Example 2. 20 is what percent of 400?

Solution: In this problem, we are looking for the percent. Use this equation:
Percent = Part ÷ Base → Percent = 20 ÷ 400 = 0.05 = 5%.
Then: 20 is 5 percent of 400.

Example 3. 70 is 25 percent of what number?

Solution: In this problem, we are looking for the base. Use this equation:
Base = Part ÷ Percent → Base = 70 ÷ 25% = 70 ÷ 0.25 = 280
Then: 70 is 25 percent of 280.

Percent of Increase and Decrease

☆ Percent of change (increase or decrease) is a mathematical concept that represents the degree of change over time.

☆ To find the percentage of increase or decrease:

1. New Number–Original Number

2. (The result÷Original Number)× 100

☆ Or use this formula: Percent of change=$\frac{new\ number - original\ number}{original\ number} \times 100$

☆ Note: If your answer is a negative number, then this is a percentage decrease. If it is positive, then this is a percentage increase.

Examples:

Example 1. The price of a shirt increases from \$40 to \$44. What is the percentage increase?

Solution: First, find the difference: 44 – 40 = 4

Then: $(4 \div 40) \times 100 = \frac{4}{40} \times 100 = 10$. The percentage increase is 10%. It means that the price of the shirt increased by 10%.

Example 2. The price of a table decreased from \$50 to \$25. What is the percent of decrease?

Solution: Use this formula:

$$Percent\ of\ change = \frac{new\ number - original\ number}{original\ number} \times 100 =$$

$\frac{25-50}{50} \times 100 = \frac{-25}{50} \times 100 = -50$. The percentage decrease is 50. (the negative sign means percentage decrease) Therefore, the price of the table decreased by 50%.

Discount, Tax and Tip

☆ To find the discount: Multiply the regular price by the rate of discount

☆ To find the selling price: Original price − discount

☆ To find tax: Multiply the tax rate to the taxable amount (income, property value, etc.)

☆ To find the tip, multiply the rate to the selling price.

Examples:

Example 1. With an 25% discount, Ella saved $50 on a dress. What was the original price of the dress?

Solution: let x be the original price of the dress. Then: 25 % of $x = 50$. Write an equation and solve for x: $0.25 \times x = 50 \rightarrow x = \frac{50}{0.25} = 200$. The original price of the dress was $200.

Example 2. Sophia purchased a new computer for a price of $820 at the Apple Store. What is the total amount her credit card is charged if the sales tax is 10%?

Solution: The taxable amount is $820, and the tax rate is 10%. Then:
$$Tax = 0.10 \times 820 = 82$$
$$Final\ price = Selling\ price + Tax \rightarrow final\ price = \$820 + \$82 = \$902$$

Example 3. Nicole and her friends went out to eat at a restaurant. If their bill was $50 and they gave their server a 12% tip, how much did they pay altogether?

Solution: First, find the tip. To find the tip, multiply the rate to the bill amount. $Tip = 50 \times 0.12 = 6$. The final amount is: $50 + $6 = $56

Simple Interest

☆ Simple Interest: The charge for borrowing money or the return for lending it.

☆ Simple interest is calculated on the initial amount (principal).

☆ To solve a simple interest problem, use this formula:

$$Interest = principal \times rate \times time \rightarrow (I = p \times r \times t = prt)$$

Examples:

Example 1. Find simple interest for $250 investment at 6% for 5 years.

Solution: Use Interest formula:
$I = prt$ ($P = \$250, r = 6\% = \frac{6}{100} = 0.06$ and $t = 5$)
Then: $I = 250 \times 0.06 \times 5 = \$75$

Example 2. Find simple interest for $1,300 at 3% for 2 years.

Solution: Use Interest formula:
$I = prt$ ($P = \$1,300, r = 3\% = \frac{3}{100} = 0.03$ and $t = 2$)
Then: $I = 1,300 \times 0.03 \times 2 = \$78.00$

Example 3. Andy received a student loan to pay for his educational expenses this year. What is the interest on the loan if he borrowed $5,100 at 5% for 4 years?

Solution: Use Interest formula: $I = prt$. $P = \$5,100$, r $= 5\% = 0.05$ and $t = 4$
Then: $I = 5,100 \times 0.05 \times 4 = \$1,020$

Example 4. Bob is starting his own small business. He borrowed $28,000 from the bank at an 7% rate for 6 months. Find the interest Bob will pay on this loan.

Solution: Use Interest formula:
$I = prt$. $P = \$28,000, r = 7\% = 0.07$ and $t = 0.5$ (6 months is half year). Then:
$I = 28,000 \times 0.07 \times 0.5 = \$980$

Day 3: Practices

✎ Reduce each ratio.

1) $3:15 =$ ___ : ___

2) $8:72 =$ ___ : ___

3) $15:25 =$ ___ : ___

4) $35:10 =$ ___ : ___

5) $36:42 =$ ___ : ___

6) $24:64 =$ ___ : ___

✎ Solve.

7) In Jack's class, 48 of the students are tall and 20 are short. In Michael's class 28 students are tall and 12 students are short. Which class has a higher ratio of tall to short students? _____

8) You can buy 7 cans of green beans at a supermarket for $7.49. How much does it cost to buy 21 cans of green beans? _____

✎ Solve each proportion.

9) $\frac{3}{4} = \frac{12}{x} \rightarrow x =$ ____

10) $\frac{2}{5} = \frac{x}{20} \rightarrow x =$ ____

11) $\frac{9}{x} = \frac{3}{5} \rightarrow x =$ ____

12) $\frac{x}{24} = \frac{5}{6} \rightarrow x =$ ____

13) $\frac{8}{4} = \frac{x}{16} \rightarrow x =$ ____

14) $\frac{3}{x} = \frac{12}{16} \rightarrow x =$ ____

15) $\frac{24}{32} = \frac{3}{x} \rightarrow x =$ ____

16) $\frac{x}{7} = \frac{21}{49} \rightarrow x =$ ____

✎ Solve each problem.

17) Two rectangles are similar. The first is 6 *feet* wide and 36 *feet* long. The second is 10 *feet* wide. What is the length of the second rectangle?

_____

18) Two rectangles are similar. One is 4.6 *meters* by 7 *meters*. The longer side of the second rectangle is 28 *meters*. What is the other side of the second rectangle? _____

✍ Solve each problem.

19) What is 15% of 60? ____

20) What is 20% of 500? ____

21) 25 what is percent of 250? __

22) 30 is what percent of 150? ___

23) 15 is 10 percent of what number? ___

24) 25 is 5 percent of what number? ___

✍ Solve each problem.

25) Bob got a raise, and his hourly wage increased from $15 to $21. What is the percent increase? ____ %

26) A $45 shirt now selling for $36 is discounted by what percent? ____ %

✍ Find the selling price of each item.

27) Original price of a computer: $500

Tax: 5%, Selling price: $_____

28) Nicolas hired a moving company. The company charged $500 for its services, and Nicolas gives the movers a 14% tip. How much does Nicolas tip the movers? $____

29) Mason has lunch at a restaurant and the cost of his meal is $60. Mason wants to leave a 10% tip. What is Mason's total bill, including tip? $_____

✍ Determine the simple interest for the following loans.

30) $800 at 3% for 2 years. $__

31) $260 at 10% for 5 years. $__

32) $380 at 4% for 3 years. $__

33) $1,200 at 2% for 1 years. $__

Day 3: Answers

1) $3:15 \rightarrow 3 \div 3 = 1,\ 15 \div 3 = 5 \rightarrow 3:15 = 1:5$

2) $8:72 \rightarrow 8 \div 8 = 1,\ 72 \div 8 = 9 \rightarrow 8:72 = 1:9$

3) $15:25 \rightarrow 15 \div 5 = 3,\ 25 \div 5 = 5 \rightarrow 15:25 = 3:5$

4) $35:10 \rightarrow 35 \div 5 = 7,\ 10 \div 5 = 2 \rightarrow 35:10 = 7:2$

5) $36:42 \rightarrow 36 \div 6 = 6,\ 42 \div 6 = 7 \rightarrow 36:42 = 6:7$

6) $24:64 \rightarrow 24 \div 8 = 3,\ 64 \div 8 = 8 \rightarrow 24:64 = 3:8$

7) In Jack's class the ratio of tall students to short students is: $\frac{48}{20} = \frac{48 \div 4}{20 \div 4} = \frac{12}{5}$ and in Michael's class the ratio is: $\frac{28}{12} = \frac{28 \div 4}{12 \div 4} = \frac{7}{3}$. Compare two fractions: $\frac{12}{5} = \frac{12 \times 3}{5 \times 3} = \frac{36}{15}$ and $\frac{7}{3} = \frac{7 \times 5}{3 \times 5} = \frac{35}{15} \rightarrow \frac{36}{15} > \frac{35}{15}$. In Jack's class the ratio of tall to short students is higher.

8) Write a proportion and solve: $\frac{7}{7.49} = \frac{21}{x} \rightarrow x = 3 \times 7.49 = \$22.47$

9) $\frac{3}{4} = \frac{12}{x} \rightarrow 3 \times x = 4 \times 12 \rightarrow 3x = 48 \rightarrow x = \frac{48}{3} = 16$

10) $\frac{2}{5} = \frac{x}{20} \rightarrow 5 \times x = 2 \times 20 \rightarrow 5x = 40 \rightarrow x = \frac{40}{5} = 8$

11) $\frac{9}{x} = \frac{3}{5} \rightarrow 9 \times 5 = 3 \times x \rightarrow 45 = 3x \rightarrow x = \frac{45}{3} = 15$

12) $\frac{x}{24} = \frac{5}{6} \rightarrow 6 \times x = 5 \times 24 \rightarrow 6x = 120 \rightarrow x = \frac{120}{6} = 20$

13) $\frac{8}{4} = \frac{x}{16} \rightarrow 8 \times 16 = 4 \times x \rightarrow 128 = 4x \rightarrow x = \frac{128}{4} = 32$

14) $\frac{3}{x} = \frac{12}{16} \rightarrow 3 \times 16 = 12 \times x \rightarrow 48 = 12x \rightarrow x = \frac{48}{12} = 4$

15) $\frac{24}{32} = \frac{3}{x} \rightarrow 24 \times x = 3 \times 32 \rightarrow 24x = 96 \rightarrow x = \frac{96}{24} = 4$

16) $\frac{x}{7} = \frac{21}{49} \rightarrow 49 \times x = 7 \times 21 \rightarrow 49x = 147 \rightarrow x = \frac{147}{49} = 3$

17) $\frac{6}{10} = \frac{36}{x} \rightarrow 6 \times x = 36 \times 10 \rightarrow 6x = 360 \rightarrow x = \frac{360}{6} = 60 \rightarrow x = 60\ feet$

18) $\frac{4.6}{7} = \frac{x}{28} \rightarrow 7 \times x = 28 \times 4.6 \rightarrow 7x = 128.8 \rightarrow x = \frac{128.8 \div 7}{7 \div 7} = 18.4 \rightarrow x =$ 18.4 $meters$

19) Part = Percent × Base → $15\% \times 60 = \frac{15}{100} \times 60 = 0.15 \times 60 = 9$

20) Part = Percent × Base → $20\% \times 500 = \frac{20}{100} \times 500 = 0.2 \times 500 = 100$

21) Percent = Part ÷ Base → $25 \div 250 = \frac{25}{250} = \frac{25 \div 25}{250 \div 25} = \frac{1}{10} = \frac{1}{10} \times 100 = 10\%$

22) Percent = Part ÷ Base → $30 \div 150 = \frac{30}{150} = \frac{30 \div 30}{150 \div 30} = \frac{1}{5} = \frac{1}{5} \times 100 = 20\%$

23) Base = Part ÷ Percent → $15 \div 10\% = 15 \div \frac{10}{100} = 15 \div 0.1 = 150$

24) Base = Part ÷ Percent → $25 \div 5\% = 25 \div \frac{5}{100} = 25 \div 0.05 = 500$

25) Percent of change $= \frac{new\ number - original\ number}{original\ number} \times 100 = \frac{21-15}{15} \times 100 = \frac{6}{15} \times 100 = 40\%$

26) $\frac{36-45}{45} \times 100 = \frac{-9}{45} \times 100 = -20\%$ (the negative sign means that the price decreased)

27) $5\% \times 500 = \frac{5}{100} \times 500 = 25 \rightarrow \$500 + \$25 = \$525$

28) $14\% \times \$500 = \frac{14}{100} \times \$500 = \$500 \times 0.14 = \$70$

29) $10\% \times \$60 = \frac{10}{100} \times \$60 = \$6 \rightarrow \$60 + \$6 = \$66$

30) $800 \times 3\% \times 2 = 800 \times \frac{3}{100} \times 2 = \frac{4,800}{100} = 48$

31) $260 \times 10\% \times 5 = 260 \times \frac{10}{100} \times 5 = 260 \times \frac{1}{10} \times 5 = 130$

32) $380 \times 4\% \times 3 = 380 \times \frac{4}{100} \times 3 = 45.6$

33) $1,200 \times 2\% \times 1 = 1,200 \times \frac{2}{100} \times 1 = 24$

DAY 4 Exponents and Variables

Math topics that you'll learn in this chapter:

1. Multiplication Property of Exponents
2. Division Property of Exponents
3. Powers of Products and Quotients
4. Zero and Negative Exponents
5. Negative Exponents and Negative Bases
6. Scientific Notation
7. Radicals

43

Multiplication Property of Exponents

☆ Exponents are shorthand for repeated multiplication of the same number by itself. For example, instead of 2×2, we can write 2^2. For $3 \times 3 \times 3 \times 3$, we can write 3^4.

☆ In algebra, a variable is a letter used to stand for a number. The most common letters are: x, y, z, a, b, c, m, and n.

☆ Exponent's rules: $x^a \times x^b = x^{a+b}$, $\frac{x^a}{x^b} = x^{a-b}$

$$(x^a)^b = x^{a \times b} \qquad (xy)^a = x^a \times y^a \qquad \left(\frac{a}{b}\right)^c = \frac{a^c}{b^c}$$

Examples:

Example 1. Multiply. $3x^2 \times 4x^3$

Solution: Use Exponent's rules: $x^a \times x^b = x^{a+b} \to x^2 \times x^3 = x^{2+3} = x^5$
Then: $3x^2 \times 4x^3 = 12x^5$

Example 2. Simplify. $(x^2 y^4)^3$

Solution: Use Exponent's rules: $(x^a)^b = x^{a \times b}$.
Then: $(x^2 y^4)^3 = x^{2 \times 3} y^{4 \times 3} = x^6 y^{12}$

Example 3. Multiply. $6x^7 \times 4x^3$

Solution: Use Exponent's rules: $x^a \times x^b = x^{a+b} \to x^7 \times x^3 = x^{7+3} = x^{10}$
Then: $6x^7 \times 4x^3 = 24x^{10}$

Example 4. Simplify. $\left(x^2 y^5\right)^4$

Solution: Use Exponent's rules: $(x^a)^b = x^{a \times b}$.
Then: $\left(x^2 y^5\right)^4 = x^{2 \times 4} y^{5 \times 4} = x^8 y^{20}$

Division Property of Exponents

For division of exponents use following formulas:

☆ $\dfrac{x^a}{x^b} = x^{a-b}$ $(x \neq 0)$

☆ $\dfrac{x^a}{x^b} = \dfrac{1}{x^{b-a}}$, $(x \neq 0)$

☆ $\dfrac{1}{x^b} = x^{-b}$

Examples:

Example 1. *Simplify.* $\dfrac{12x^2y}{3xy^3} =$

Solution: First, cancel the common factor: $3 \to \dfrac{12x^2y}{3xy^3} = \dfrac{4x^2y}{xy^3}$

Use Exponent's rules: $\dfrac{x^a}{x^b} = x^{a-b} \to \dfrac{x^2}{x} = x^{2-1} = x^1$ and $\dfrac{x^a}{x^b} = \dfrac{1}{x^{b-a}} \to \dfrac{y}{y^3} = \dfrac{1}{y^{3-1}} = \dfrac{1}{y^2}$

Then: $\dfrac{12x^2y}{3xy^3} = \dfrac{4x}{y^2}$

Example 2. *Simplify.* $\dfrac{48x^{12}}{16x^9} =$

Solution: Use Exponent's rules: $\dfrac{x^a}{x^b} = x^{a-b} \to \dfrac{x^{12}}{x^9} = x^{12-9} = x^3$

Then: $\dfrac{48x^{12}}{16x^9} = 3x^3$

Example 3. *Simplify.* $\dfrac{6x^5y^7}{42x^8y^2} =$

Solution: First, cancel the common factor: $6 \to \dfrac{x^5y^7}{7x^8y^2}$

Use Exponent's rules: $\dfrac{x^a}{x^b} = x^{a-b} \to \dfrac{x^5}{x^8} = x^{5-8} = x^{-3} = \dfrac{1}{x^3}$ and $\dfrac{y^7}{y^2} = y^{7-2} = y^5$

Then: $\dfrac{6x^5y^7}{42x^8y^2} = \dfrac{y^5}{7x^3}$

Powers of Products and Quotients

☆ For any nonzero numbers a and b and any integer x, $(ab)^x = a^x \times b^x$

and $\left(\frac{a}{b}\right)^c = \frac{a^c}{b^c}$

Examples:

Example 1. Simplify. $\left(6x^4y^5\right)^2$

Solution: Use Exponent's rules: $(x^a)^b = x^{a \times b}$

$\left(6x^4y^5\right)^2 = (6)^2(x^4)^2\left(y^5\right)^2 = 36x^{4 \times 2}y^{5 \times 2} = 36x^8y^{10}$

Example 2. Simplify. $\left(\frac{5x^5}{2x^4}\right)^2$

Solution: First, cancel the common factor: $x^4 \rightarrow \left(\frac{5x^5}{2x^4}\right) = \left(\frac{5x}{2}\right)^2$

Use Exponent's rules: $\left(\frac{a}{b}\right)^c = \frac{a^c}{b^c}$. Then: $\left(\frac{5x}{2}\right)^2 = \frac{(5x)^2}{(2)^2} = \frac{25x^2}{4}$

Example 3. Simplify. $(-6x^7y^3)^2$

Solution: Use Exponent's rules: $(x^a)^b = x^{a \times b}$

$(-6x^7y^3)^2 = (-6)^2(x^7)^2(y^3)^2 = 36x^{7 \times 2}y^{3 \times 2} = 36x^{14}y^6$

Example 4. Simplify. $\left(\frac{8x^3}{5x^7}\right)^2$

Solution: First, cancel the common factor: $x^3 \rightarrow \left(\frac{8x^3}{5x^7}\right)^2 = \left(\frac{8}{5x^4}\right)^2$

Use Exponent's rules: $\left(\frac{a}{b}\right)^c = \frac{a^c}{b^c}$, Then: $\left(\frac{8}{5x^4}\right)^2 = \frac{8^2}{(5x^4)^2} = \frac{64}{25x^8}$

Zero and Negative Exponents

☆ Zero-Exponent Rule: $a^0 = 1$, this means that anything raised to the zero power is 1. For example: $(5xy)^0 = 1$ (number zero is an exception: $0^0 = 0$)

☆ A negative exponent simply means that the base is on the wrong side of the fraction line, so you need to flip the base to the other side. For instance, "x^{-2}" (pronounced as "ecks to the minus two") just means "x^2" but underneath, as in $\frac{1}{x^2}$.

Examples:

Example 1. Evaluate. $\left(\frac{3}{7}\right)^{-2} =$

Solution: Use negative exponent's rule: $\left(\frac{x^a}{x^b}\right)^{-2} = \left(\frac{x^b}{x^a}\right)^{2} \rightarrow \left(\frac{3}{7}\right)^{-2} = \left(\frac{7}{3}\right)^{2}$
Then: $\left(\frac{7}{3}\right)^{2} = \frac{7^2}{3^2} = \frac{49}{9}$

Example 2. Evaluate. $\left(\frac{2}{5}\right)^{-3} =$

Solution: Use negative exponent's rule: $\left(\frac{x^a}{x^b}\right)^{-3} = \left(\frac{x^b}{x^a}\right)^{3} \rightarrow \left(\frac{2}{5}\right)^{-3} = \left(\frac{5}{2}\right)^{3} =$
Then: $\left(\frac{5}{2}\right)^{3} = \frac{5^3}{2^3} = \frac{125}{8}$

Example 3. Evaluate. $\left(\frac{a}{b}\right)^{0} =$

Solution: Use zero-exponent Rule: $a^0 = 1$
Then: $\left(\frac{a}{b}\right)^{0} = 1$

Example 4. Evaluate. $\left(\frac{9}{5}\right)^{-1} =$

Solution: Use negative exponent's rule: $\left(\frac{x^a}{x^b}\right)^{-1} = \left(\frac{x^b}{x^a}\right)^{1} \rightarrow \left(\frac{9}{5}\right)^{-1} = \left(\frac{5}{9}\right)^{1} = \frac{5}{9}$

Negative Exponents and Negative Bases

☆ A negative exponent is the reciprocal of that number with a positive exponent. $(3)^{-2} = \frac{1}{3^2}$

☆ To simplify a negative exponent, make the power positive!

☆ The parenthesis is important! -5^{-2} is not the same as $(-5)^{-2}$

$$-5^{-2} = -\frac{1}{5^2} \text{ and } (-5)^{-2} = +\frac{1}{5^2}$$

Examples:

Example 1. *Simplify.* $\left(\frac{4a}{7c}\right)^{-2} =$

Solution: Use negative exponent's rule: $\left(\frac{x^a}{x^b}\right)^{-2} = \left(\frac{x^b}{x^a}\right)^{2} \rightarrow \left(\frac{4a}{7c}\right)^{-2} = \left(\frac{7c}{4a}\right)^{2}$

Now use exponent's rule: $\left(\frac{a}{b}\right)^c = \frac{a^c}{b^c} \rightarrow \left(\frac{7c}{4a}\right)^2 = \frac{7^2c^2}{4^2a^2}$

Then: $\frac{7^2c^2}{4^2a^2} = \frac{49c^2}{16a^2}$

Example 2. *Simplify.* $\left(\frac{3x}{y}\right)^{-3} =$

Solution: Use negative exponent's rule: $\left(\frac{x^a}{x^b}\right)^{-3} = \left(\frac{x^b}{x^a}\right)^{3} \rightarrow \left(\frac{3x}{y}\right)^{-3} = \left(\frac{y}{3x}\right)^{3}$

Now use exponent's rule: $\left(\frac{a}{b}\right)^c = \frac{a^c}{b^c} \rightarrow \left(\frac{y}{3x}\right)^3 = \frac{y^3}{3^3x^3} = \frac{y^3}{27x^3}$

Example 3. *Simplify.* $\left(\frac{7a}{4c}\right)^{-2} =$

Solution: Use negative exponent's rule: $\left(\frac{x^a}{x^b}\right)^{-2} = \left(\frac{x^b}{x^a}\right)^{2} \rightarrow \left(\frac{7a}{4c}\right)^{-2} = \left(\frac{4c}{7a}\right)^{2}$

Now use exponent's rule: $\left(\frac{a}{b}\right)^c = \frac{a^c}{b^c} \rightarrow \left(\frac{4c}{7a}\right)^2 = \frac{4^2c^2}{7^2a^2}$

Then: $\frac{4^2c^2}{7^2a^2} = \frac{16c^2}{49a^2}$

Scientific Notation

✭ Scientific notation is used to write very big or very small numbers in decimal form.

✭ In scientific notation, all numbers are written in the form of: $m \times 10^n$, where m is greater than 1 and less than 10.

✭ To convert a number from scientific notation to standard form, move the decimal point to the left (if the exponent of ten is a negative number), or to the right (if the exponent is positive).

Examples:

Example 1. *Write* 0.000037 *in scientific notation.*

Solution: First, move the decimal point to the right so you have a number between 1 and 10. That number is 3.7. Now, determine how many places the decimal moved in step 1 by the power of 10. We moved the decimal point 5 digits to the right. Then: 10^{-5}. When the decimal moved to the right, the exponent is negative. Then: $0.000037 = 3.7 \times 10^{-5}$

Example 2. *Write* 5.3×10^{-3} *in standard notation.*

Solution: The exponent is negative 3. Then, move the decimal point to the left three digits. (remember 5.3 = 0000005.3) When the decimal moved to the right, the exponent is negative. Then: $5.3 \times 10^{-3} = 0.0053$

Example 3. *Write* 0.00042 *in scientific notation.*

Solution: First, move the decimal point to the right so you have a number between 1 and 10. Then: $m = 4.2$. Now, determine how many places the decimal moved in step 1 by the power of 10. 10^{-4}. Then: $0.00042 = 4.2 \times 10^{-4}$

Example 4. *Write* 7.3×10^7 *in standard notation.*

Solution: The exponent is positive 7. Then, move the decimal point to the right seven digits. (remember 7.3 = 7.3000000) Then: $7.3 \times 10^7 = 73,000,000$

Radicals

☆ If n is a positive integer and x is a real number, then: $\sqrt[n]{x} = x^{\frac{1}{n}}$,

$$\sqrt[n]{xy} = x^{\frac{1}{n}} \times y^{\frac{1}{n}}, \sqrt[n]{\frac{x}{y}} = \frac{x^{\frac{1}{n}}}{y^{\frac{1}{n}}}, \text{ and } \sqrt[n]{x} \times \sqrt[n]{y} = \sqrt[n]{xy}$$

☆ A square root of x is a number r whose square is: $r^2 = x$ (r is a square root of x)

☆ To add and subtract radicals, we need to have the same values under the radical. For example: $\sqrt{5} + 3\sqrt{5} = 4\sqrt{5}$, $5\sqrt{6} - 2\sqrt{6} = 3\sqrt{5}$

Examples:

Example 1. Find the square root of $\sqrt{256}$.

Solution: First, factor the number: $256 = 16^2$. Then: $\sqrt{256} = \sqrt{16^2}$
Now use radical rule: $\sqrt[n]{a^n} = a$. Then: $\sqrt{256} = \sqrt{16^2} = 16$

Example 2. Evaluate. $\sqrt{9} \times \sqrt{36} =$

Solution: Find the values of $\sqrt{9}$ and $\sqrt{36}$. Then: $\sqrt{9} \times \sqrt{36} = 3 \times 6 = 18$

Example 3. Solve. $3\sqrt{7} + 11\sqrt{7}$.

Solution: Since we have the same values under the radical, we can add these two radicals: $3\sqrt{7} + 11\sqrt{7} = 14\sqrt{7}$

Example 4. Evaluate. $\sqrt{40} \times \sqrt{10} =$

Solution: Use this radical rule: $\sqrt[n]{x} \times \sqrt[n]{y} = \sqrt[n]{xy} \rightarrow \sqrt{40} \times \sqrt{10} = \sqrt{400}$
The square root of 400 is 20. Then: $\sqrt{40} \times \sqrt{10} = \sqrt{400} = 20$

Day 4: Practices

✍ Find the products.

1) $5x^3 \times 2x =$

2) $x^4 \times 5x^2y =$

3) $2xy \times 3x^5y^2 =$

4) $4xy^2 \times 2x^2y =$

5) $-3x^3y^3 \times 2x^2y^2 =$

6) $-5xy^2 \times 3x^5y^2 =$

7) $-5x^2y^6 \times 6x^5y^2 =$

8) $-2x^3y^3 \times 2x^3y^3 =$

9) $-7xy^3 \times 4x^5y^2 =$

10) $-x^4y^3 \times (-5x^6y^2) =$

11) $-6y^6 \times 7x^6y^2 =$

12) $-8x^4 \times 2y^2 =$

✍ Simplify.

13) $\frac{3^2 \times 3^3}{3^3 \times 3} =$

14) $\frac{4^2 \times 4^4}{5^4 \times 5} =$

15) $\frac{14x^5}{7x^2} =$

16) $\frac{15x^3}{5x^6} =$

17) $\frac{64y^3}{8xy^7} =$

18) $\frac{10x^4y^5}{30x^5y^4} =$

19) $\frac{11y}{44x^3y^3} =$

20) $\frac{40xy^3}{120xy^3} =$

21) $\frac{45x^3}{25xy^3} =$

22) $\frac{72y^6x}{36x^8y^9} =$

✍ Solve.

23) $(x^2 \, y^2)^3 =$

24) $(2x^3 \, y^2)^3 =$

25) $(2x \times 3xy^2)^2 =$

26) $(4x \times 2y^4)^2 =$

27) $\left(\frac{3x}{x^2}\right)^2 =$

28) $\left(\frac{6y}{18y^3}\right)^2 =$

29) $\left(\frac{3x^2y^2}{12x^4y^3}\right)^3 =$

30) $\left(\frac{23x^5y^3}{46x^3y^5}\right)^3 =$

31) $\left(\frac{16x^7y^3}{48x^5y^2}\right)^2 =$

32) $\left(\frac{12x^5y^6}{60x^7y^2}\right)^2 =$

✎ **Evaluate each expression. (Zero and Negative Exponents)**

33) $\left(\frac{1}{3}\right)^{-2} =$

36) $\left(\frac{2}{3}\right)^{-3} =$

34) $\left(\frac{1}{4}\right)^{-3} =$

37) $\left(\frac{2}{5}\right)^{-3} =$

35) $\left(\frac{1}{6}\right)^{-2} =$

38) $\left(\frac{3}{5}\right)^{-2} =$

✎ **Write each expression with positive exponents.**

39) $2y^{-3} =$

43) $23a^2b^{-4}c^{-8} =$

40) $13y^{-5} =$

44) $-4x^4y^{-2} =$

41) $-20x^{-2} =$

45) $\frac{16y}{x^3y^{-4}} =$

42) $15a^{-2}b^3 =$

46) $\frac{30a^{-3}b}{-100c^{-2}} =$

✎ **Write each number in scientific notation.**

47) $0.00518 =$

49) $78,000 =$

48) $0.000042 =$

50) $92,000,000 =$

✎ **Evaluate.**

51) $\sqrt{5} \times \sqrt{5} =$

55) $\sqrt{2} \times \sqrt{18} =$

52) $\sqrt{25} - \sqrt{4} =$

56) $4\sqrt{2} + 3\sqrt{2} =$

53) $\sqrt{81} + \sqrt{36} =$

57) $5\sqrt{7} + 2\sqrt{7} =$

54) $\sqrt{4} \times \sqrt{25} =$

58) $\sqrt{45} + 2\sqrt{5} =$

Day 4: Answers

1) $5x^3 \times 2x \to x^3 \times x^1 = x^{3+1} = x^4 \to 5x^3 \times 2x = 10x^4$

2) $x^4 \times 5x^2 y \to x^4 \times x^2 = x^{4+2} = x^6 \to x^4 \times 5x^2 y = 5x^6 y$

3) $2xy \times 3x^5 y^2 \to x \times x^5 = x^{1+5} = x^6, \ y \times y^2 = y^{1+2} = y^3 \to 2xy \times 3x^5 y^2 = 6x^6 y^3$

4) $4xy^2 \times 2x^2 y \to x \times x^2 = x^{1+2} = x^3, \ y^2 \times y = y^{2+1} = y^3 \to 4xy^2 \times 2x^2 y = 8x^3 y^3$

5) $-3x^3 y^3 \times 2x^2 y^2 \to x^3 \times x^2 = x^{3+2} = x^5, \ y^3 \times y^2 = y^{3+2} = y^5 \to$

   $-3x^3 y^3 \times 2x^2 y^2 = -6x^5 y^5$

6) $-5xy^2 \times 3x^5 y^2 \to x \times x^5 = x^{1+5} = x^6, \ y^2 \times y^2 = y^{2+2} = y^4 \to$

   $-5xy^2 \times 3x^5 y^2 = -15x^6 y^4$

7) $-5x^2 y^6 \times 6x^5 y^2 \to x^2 \times x^5 = x^{2+5} = x^7, \ y^6 \times y^2 = y^{6+2} = y^8 \to$

   $-5x^2 y^6 \times 6x^5 y^2 = -30x^7 y^8$

8) $-2x^3 y^3 \times 2x^3 y^3 \to x^3 \times x^3 = x^{3+3} = x^6, \ y^3 \times y^3 = y^{3+3} = y^6 \to$

   $-2x^3 y^3 \times 2x^3 y^3 = -4x^6 y^6$

9) $-7xy^3 \times 4x^5 y^2 \to x \times x^5 = x^{1+5} = x^6, \ y^3 \times y^2 = y^{3+2} = y^5 \to$

   $-7xy^3 \times 4x^5 y^2 = -28x^6 y^5$

10) $-x^4 y^3 \times (-5x^6 y^2) \to x^4 \times x^6 = x^{4+6} = x^{10}, \ y^3 \times y^2 = y^{3+2} = y^5 \to$

   $-x^4 y^3 \times (-5x^6 y^2) = 5x^{10} y^5$

11) $-6y^6 \times 7x^6 y^2 \to y^6 \times y^2 = y^{6+2} = y^8 \to -6y^6 \times 7x^6 y^2 = -42x^6 y^8$

12) $-8x^4 \times 2y^2 = -16x^4 y^2$

13) $\frac{3^2 \times 3^3}{3^3 \times 3} = \frac{3^{2+3}}{3^{3+1}} = \frac{3^5}{3^4} = 3^{5-4} = 3^1 = 3$

14) $\frac{4^2 \times 4^4}{5^4 \times 5} = \frac{4^{2+4}}{5^{4+1}} = \frac{4^6}{5^5}$

15) $\frac{14x^5}{7x^2} \to \frac{14 \div 7}{7 \div 7} = 2, \ \frac{x^5}{x^2} = x^{5-2} = x^3 \to \frac{14x^5}{7x^2} = 2x^3$

16) $\frac{15x^3}{5x^6} \to \frac{15 \div 5}{5 \div 5} = 3, \ \frac{x^3}{x^6} = x^{3-6} = x^{-3} = \frac{1}{x^3} \to \frac{15x^3}{5x^6} = \frac{3}{x^3}$

17) $\frac{64y^3}{8xy^7} \to \frac{64 \div 8}{8 \div 8} = 8, \ \frac{y^3}{y^7} = y^{3-7} = y^{-4} = \frac{1}{y^4} \to \frac{64y^3}{8xy^7} = \frac{8}{xy^4}$

18) $\frac{10x^4 y^5}{30x^5 y^4} \to \frac{10 \div 10}{30 \div 10} = \frac{1}{3}, \ \frac{x^4}{x^5} = x^{4-5} = x^{-1} = \frac{1}{x}, \ \frac{y^5}{y^4} = y^{5-4} = y^1 \to \frac{10x^4 y^5}{30x^5 y^4} = \frac{y}{3x}$

19) $\frac{11y}{44x^3y^3} \rightarrow \frac{11\div11}{44\div11} = \frac{1}{4}, \frac{y}{y^3} = y^{1-3} = y^{-2} = \frac{1}{y^2} \rightarrow \frac{11y}{44x^3y^3} = \frac{1}{4x^3y^2}$

20) $\frac{40xy^3}{120xy^3} \rightarrow \frac{40\div40}{120\div40} = \frac{1}{3}, \frac{x}{x} = x^{1-1} = x^0 = 1, \frac{y^3}{y^3} = y^{3-3} = y^0 = 1 \rightarrow \frac{40xy^3}{120xy^3} = \frac{1}{3}$

21) $\frac{45x^3}{25xy^3} \rightarrow \frac{45\div5}{25\div5} = \frac{9}{5}, \frac{x^3}{x} = x^{3-1} = x^2 \rightarrow \frac{45x^3}{25xy^3} = \frac{9x^2}{5y^3}$

22) $\frac{72y^6x}{36x^8y^9} \rightarrow \frac{72\div36}{36\div36} = \frac{2}{1} = 2, \frac{y^6}{y^9} = y^{6-9} = y^{-3} = \frac{1}{y^3}, \frac{x}{x^8} = x^{1-8} = x^{-7} = \frac{1}{x^7} \rightarrow \frac{72y^6x}{36x^8y^9} = \frac{2}{x^7y^3}$

23) $(x^2\,y^2)^3 = x^{2\times3}\,y^{2\times3} = x^6\,y^6$

24) $(2x^3\,y^2)^3 = 2^3x^{3\times3}\,y^{2\times3} = 8x^9y^6$

25) $(2x \times 3xy^2)^2 = (2\times3)^2x^{(1+1)\times2}\,y^{2\times2} = 6^2x^{2\times2}\,y^4 = 36x^4\,y^4$

26) $(4x \times 2y^4)^2 = (4\times2)^2x^{1\times2}\,y^{4\times2} = 8^2x^2\,y^8 = 64x^2\,y^8$

27) $\left(\frac{3x}{x^2}\right)^2 = \frac{3^{1\times2}x^{1\times2}}{x^{2\times2}} = \frac{3^2x^2}{x^4} \rightarrow 3^2 = 9, \frac{x^2}{x^4} = x^{2-4} = x^{-2} = \frac{1}{x^2} \rightarrow \left(\frac{3x}{x^2}\right)^2 = \frac{9}{x^2}$

28) $\left(\frac{6y}{18y^3}\right)^2 = \frac{6^{1\times2}y^{1\times2}}{(18)^{1\times2}y^{3\times2}} = \frac{6^2y^2}{18^2y^6} \rightarrow \frac{36}{324} = \frac{1}{9}, \frac{y^2}{y^6} = y^{2-6} = y^{-4} = \frac{1}{y^4} \rightarrow \left(\frac{6y}{18y^3}\right)^2 = \frac{1}{9y^4}$

29) $\left(\frac{3x^2y^2}{12x^4y^3}\right)^3 = \frac{3^{1\times3}x^{2\times3}y^{2\times3}}{(12)^{1\times3}x^{4\times3}y^{3\times3}} = \frac{3^3x^6y^6}{12^3x^{12}y^9} \rightarrow \frac{3^3}{12^3} = \frac{27}{1,728} = \frac{1}{64}, \frac{x^6}{x^{12}} = x^{6-12} = x^{-6} = \frac{1}{x^6}, \frac{y^6}{y^9} =$

$y^{6-9} = y^{-3} = \frac{1}{y^3} \rightarrow \left(\frac{3x^2y^2}{12x^4y^3}\right)^3 = \frac{1}{64x^6y^3}$

30) $\left(\frac{23x^5y^3}{46x^3y^5}\right)^3 = \frac{23^{1\times3}x^{5\times3}y^{3\times3}}{(23\times2)^{1\times3}x^{3\times3}y^{5\times3}} = \frac{23^3x^{15}y^9}{23^3\times2^3x^9y^{15}} = \frac{x^{15}y^9}{8x^9y^{15}} \rightarrow \frac{x^{15}}{x^9} = x^{15-9} = x^6, \frac{y^9}{y^{15}} = y^{9-15} =$

$y^{-6} = \frac{1}{y^6} \rightarrow \left(\frac{23x^5y^3}{46x^3y^5}\right)^3 = \frac{x^6}{8y^6}$

31) $\left(\frac{16x^7y^3}{48x^5y^2}\right)^2 = \frac{16^{1\times2}x^{7\times2}y^{3\times2}}{(16\times3)^{1\times2}x^{5\times2}y^{2\times2}} = \frac{16^2x^{14}y^6}{16^2\times3^2x^{10}y^4} = \frac{x^{14}y^6}{9x^{10}y^4} \rightarrow \frac{x^{14}}{x^{10}} = x^{14-10} = x^4, \frac{y^6}{y^4} = y^{6-4} =$

$y^2 \rightarrow \left(\frac{16x^7y^3}{48x^5y^2}\right)^2 = \frac{x^4y^2}{9}$

32) $\left(\frac{12x^5y^6}{60x^7y^2}\right)^2 = \frac{12^{1\times2}x^{5\times2}y^{6\times2}}{(12\times5)^{1\times2}x^{7\times2}y^{2\times2}} = \frac{12^2x^{10}y^{12}}{12^2\times5^2x^{14}y^4} = \frac{x^{10}y^{12}}{25x^{14}y^4} \rightarrow \frac{x^{10}}{x^{14}} = x^{10-14} = x^{-4} = \frac{1}{x^4}, \frac{y^{12}}{y^4} =$

$y^{12-4} = y^8 \rightarrow \left(\frac{12x^5y^6}{60x^7y^2}\right)^2 = \frac{y^8}{25x^4}$

33) $\left(\frac{1}{3}\right)^{-2} = 3^2 = 9$ 34) $\left(\frac{1}{4}\right)^{-3} = 4^3 = 64$

35) $\left(\frac{1}{6}\right)^{-2} = 6^2 = 36$

36) $\left(\frac{2}{3}\right)^{-3} = \left(\frac{3}{2}\right)^3 = \frac{3^3}{2^3} = \frac{27}{8}$

37) $\left(\frac{2}{5}\right)^{-3} = \left(\frac{5}{2}\right)^3 = \frac{5^3}{2^3} = \frac{125}{8}$

38) $\left(\frac{3}{5}\right)^{-2} = \left(\frac{5}{3}\right)^2 = \frac{5^2}{3^2} = \frac{25}{9}$

39) $2y^{-3} = \frac{2}{y^3}$

40) $13y^{-5} = \frac{13}{y^5}$

41) $-20x^{-2} = -\frac{20}{x^2}$

42) $15a^{-2}b^3 = \frac{15b^3}{a^2}$

43) $23a^2b^{-4}c^{-8} = \frac{23a^2}{b^4c^8}$

44) $-4x^4y^{-2}2^{-7} = -\frac{4x^4}{y^2}$

45) $\frac{16y}{x^3y^{-4}} \rightarrow \frac{y}{y^{-4}} = y^{1-(-4)} = y^5 \rightarrow \frac{16y}{x^3y^{-4}} = \frac{16y^5}{x^3}$

46) $\frac{30a^{-3}b}{-100c^{-2}} \rightarrow -\frac{30 \div 10}{100 \div 10} = -\frac{3}{10} \rightarrow \frac{30a^{-3}b}{-100c^{-2}} = -\frac{3c^2b}{10a^3}$

47) $0.00518 = 5.18 \times 10^{-3}$

48) $0.000042 = 4.2 \times 10^{-5}$

49) $78,000 = 7.8 \times 10^4$

50) $92,000,000 = 9.2 \times 10^7$

51) $\sqrt{5} \times \sqrt{5} = \sqrt{25} = 5$

52) $\sqrt{25} - \sqrt{4} = 5 - 2 = 3$

53) $\sqrt{81} + \sqrt{36} = 9 + 6 = 15$

54) $\sqrt{4} \times \sqrt{25} = 2 + 5 = 10$

55) $\sqrt{2} \times \sqrt{18} = \sqrt{36} = 6$

56) $4\sqrt{2} + 3\sqrt{2} = 7\sqrt{2}$

57) $5\sqrt{7} + 2\sqrt{7} = 7\sqrt{7}$

58) $\sqrt{45} + 2\sqrt{5} = \sqrt{5 \times 9} + 2\sqrt{5} = 3\sqrt{5} + 2\sqrt{5} = 5\sqrt{5}$

Expressions and Variables

Math topics that you'll learn in this chapter:

1. Simplifying Variable Expressions
2. Simplifying Polynomial Expressions
3. The Distributive Property
4. Evaluating One Variable
5. Evaluating Two Variables

57

Simplifying Variable Expressions

☆ In algebra, a variable is a letter used to stand for a number. The most common letters are $x, y, z, a, b, c, m,$ and n.

☆ An algebraic expression is an expression that contains integers, variables, and math operations such as addition, subtraction, multiplication, division, etc.

☆ In an expression, we can combine "like" terms. (values with same variable and same power)

Examples:

Example 1. Simplify. $(3x + 9x + 2) =$

Solution: In this expression, there are three terms: $3x,\ 9x,$ and 2. Two terms are "like terms": $3x$ and $9x$. Combine like terms. $3x + 9x = 12x$. Then: $(3x + 9x + 2) = 12x + 2$ (***remember you cannot combine variables and numbers.***)

Example 2. Simplify. $-17x^2 + 6x + 15x^2 - 13 =$

Solution: Combine "like" terms: $-17x^2 + 15x^2 = -2x^2$
Then: $-17x^2 + 6x + 15x^2 - 13 = -2x^2 + 6x - 13$

Example 3. Simplify. $5x - 18 - 6x^2 + 3x^2 =$

Solution: Combine like terms. Then:
$5x - 18 - 6x^2 + 3x^2 = -3x^2 + 5x - 18$

Example 4. Simplify. $-5x - 4x^2 + 9x - 11x^2 =$
Solution: Combine "like" terms: $-5x + 9x = 4x,$ and $-4x^2 - 11x^2 = -15x^2$
Then: $-5x - 4x^2 + 9x - 11x^2 = 4x - 15x^2$. Write in standard form (biggest powers first): $4x - 15x^2 = -15x^2 + 4x$

Simplifying Polynomial Expressions

☆ In mathematics, a polynomial is an expression consisting of variables and coefficients that involves only the operations of addition, subtraction, multiplication, and non–negative integer exponents of variables.

$$P(x) = a_n x^n + a_{n-1} x^{n-1} + \dots + a_2 x^2 + a_1 x + a_0$$

☆ Polynomials must always be simplified as much as possible. It means you must add together any like terms. (values with same variable and same power)

Examples:

Example 1. Simplify this Polynomial Expressions. $-2x^2 + 9x^3 + 5x^3 - 7x^4$

Solution: Combine "like" terms: $9x^3 + 5x^3 = 14x^3$

Then: $-2x^2 + 9x^3 + 5x^3 - 7x^4 = -2x^2 + 14x^3 - 7x^4$
Now, write the expression in standard form:
$-2x^2 + 14x^3 - 7x^4 = -7x^4 + 14x^3 - 2x^2$

Example 2. Simplify this expression. $(4x^2 - x^3) - (-6x^3 + 3x^2) =$

Solution: First, multiply $(-)$ into $(-6x^3 + 3x^2)$:

$(4x^2 - x^3) - (-6x^3 + 3x^2) = 4x^2 - x^3 + 6x^3 - 3x^2$
Then combine "like" terms: $4x^2 - x^3 + 6x^3 - 3x^2 = x^2 + 5x^3$
And write in standard form: $x^2 + 5x^3 = 5x^3 + x^2$

Example 3. Simplify. $-2x^3 + 6x^4 - 5x^2 - 14x^4 =$

Solution: Combine "like" terms: $6x^4 - 14x^4 = -8x^4$
Then: $-2x^3 + 6x^4 - 5x^2 - 14x^4 = -2x^3 - 8x^4 - 5x^2$
And write in standard form: $-2x^3 - 8x^4 - 5x^2 = -8x^4 - 2x^3 - 5x^2$

The Distributive Property

✪ The distributive property (or the distributive property of multiplication over addition and subtraction) simplifies and solves expressions in the form of: $a(b + c)$ or $a(b - c)$

✪ The distributive property is multiplying a term outside the parentheses by the terms inside.

✪ Distributive Property rule: $a(b + c) = ab + ac$

Examples:

Example 1. Simply using the distributive property. $(3)(4x - 9)$

Solution: Use Distributive Property rule: $a(b + c) = ab + ac$

$(3)(4x - 9) = (3 \times 4x) + (3) \times (-9) = 12x - 27$

Example 2. Simply. $(-4)(-3x + 8)$

Solution: Use Distributive Property rule: $a(b + c) = ab + ac$

$(-4)(-3x + 8) = (-4 \times (-3x)) + (-4) \times (8) = 12x - 32$

Example 3. Simply. $(5)(3x + 4) - 13x$

Solution: First, simplify $(5)(3x + 4)$ using the distributive property.

Then: $(5)(3x + 4) = 15x + 20$

Now combine like terms: $(5)(3x + 4) - 13x = 15x + 20 - 13x$

In this expression, $15x$ and $-13x$ are "like terms" and we can combine them.

$15x - 13x = 2x$. Then: $15x + 20 - 13x = 2x + 20$

Evaluating One Variable

☆ To evaluate one variable expressions, find the variable and substitute a number for that variable.

☆ Perform the arithmetic operations.

Examples:

Example 1. Calculate this expression for $x = 1$. $9 + 8x$

Solution: First, substitute 1 for x.

Then: $9 + 8x = 9 + 8(1)$

Now, use order of operation to find the answer: $9 + 8(1) = 9 + 8 = 17$

Example 2. Evaluate this expression for $x = -2$. $7x - 3$

Solution: First, substitute -2 for x.

Then: $7x - 3 = 7(-2) - 3$

Now, use order of operation to find the answer: $7(-2) - 3 = -14 - 3 = -17$

Example 3. Find the value of this expression when $x = 3$. $(12 - 2x)$

Solution: First, substitute 3 for x,

Then: $12 - 2x = 12 - 2(3) = 12 - 6 = 6$

Example 4. Solve this expression for $x = -4$. $11 + 5x$

Solution: Substitute -4 for x.

Then: $11 + 5x = 11 + 5(-4) = 11 - 20 = -9$

Evaluating Two Variables

✰ To evaluate an algebraic expression, substitute a number for each variable.

✰ Perform the arithmetic operations to find the value of the expression.

Examples:

Example 1. Calculate this expression for $a = -2$ and $b = 3$. $(2a - 6b)$

Solution: First, substitute -2 for a, and 3 for b.
Then: $2a - 6b = 2(-2) - 6(3)$
Now, use order of operation to find the answer: $2(-2) - 6(3) = -4 - 18 = -22$

Example 2. Evaluate this expression for $x = -3$ and $y = 4$. $(2x - 4y)$

Solution: Substitute -3 for x, and 4 for y.
Then: $2x - 4y = 2(-3) - 4(4) = -6 - 16 = -22$

Example 3. Find the value of this expression $3(-4a + 2b)$, when $a = -2$ and $b = -3$.

Solution: Substitute -2 for a, and -3 for b.
Then: $3(-4a + 2b) = 3\big(-4(-2) + 2(-3)\big) = 3(8 - 6) = 3(2) = 6$

Example 4. Evaluate this expression. $-5x - 3y$, $x = 2$, $y = -6$

Solution: Substitute 2 for x, and -6 for y and simplify.
Then: $-5x - 3y = -5(2) - 3(-6) = -10 + 18 = 8$

Day 5: Practices

✎ Simplify each expression.

1) $2 - 3x - 1 =$

2) $-6 - 2x + 8 =$

3) $11x - 6x - 4 =$

4) $-16x + 25x - 5 =$

5) $5x + 5 - 15x =$

6) $4 + 5x - 6x - 5 =$

7) $3x + 10 - 2x - 20 =$

8) $-3 - 2x^2 - 5 + 3x =$

9) $-7 + 9x^2 - 2 + 2x =$

10) $4x^2 + 2x - 12x - 5 =$

11) $2x^2 - 3x - 5x + 6 - 9 =$

12) $x^2 - 6x - x + 2 - 3 =$

13) $10x^2 - x - 8x + 3 - 10 =$

14) $4x^2 - 7x - x^2 + 2x + 5 =$

✎ Simplify each polynomial.

15) $4x^2 + 3x^3 - x^2 + x =$

16) $5x^4 + x^5 - x^4 + 4x^2 =$

17) $15x^3 + 12x - 6x^2 - 9x^3 =$

18) $(7x^3 - 2x^2) + (6x^2 - 13x) =$

19) $(9x^4 + 6x^3) + (11x^3 - 5x^4) =$

20) $(15x^5 - 5x^3) - (4x^3 + 6x^2) =$

21) $(15x^4 + 7x^3) - (3x^3 - 26) =$

22) $(22x^4 + 6x^3) - (-2x^3 - 4x^4) =$

23) $(x^2 + 6x^3) + (-19x^2 + 6x^3) =$

24) $(2x^4 - x^3) + (-5x^3 - 7x^4) =$

✍ Use the distributive property to simply each expression.

25) $3(5 + x) =$

26) $5(4 - x) =$

27) $6(2 - 5x) =$

28) $(4 - 3x)7 =$

29) $8(3 - 3x) =$

30) $(-1)(-6 + 2x) =$

31) $(-5)(3x - 3) =$

32) $(-x + 10)(-3)$

33) $(-2)(2 - 6x) =$

34) $(-6x - 4)(-7) =$

✍ Evaluate each expression using the value given.

35) $x = 3 \rightarrow 12 - x =$

36) $x = 5 \rightarrow x + 7 =$

37) $x = 3 \rightarrow 3x - 5 =$

38) $x = 2 \rightarrow 18 - 3x =$

39) $x = 7 \rightarrow 5x - 4 =$

40) $x = 6 \rightarrow 21 - x =$

41) $x = 5 \rightarrow 10x - 20 =$

42) $x = -5 \rightarrow 4 - x =$

43) $x = -2 \rightarrow 25 - 3x =$

44) $x = -7 \rightarrow 16 - x =$

45) $x = -13 \rightarrow 40 - 2x =$

46) $x = -4 \rightarrow 20x - 6 =$

47) $x = -6 \rightarrow -11x - 19 =$

48) $x = -8 \rightarrow -1 - 3x =$

✍ Evaluate each expression using the values given.

49) $x = 3, \ y = 2 \rightarrow 3x + 2y =$

50) $a = 4, \ b = 1 \rightarrow 2a - 6b =$

51) $x = 5, \ y = 7 \rightarrow 2x - 4y - 5 =$

52) $a = -3, \ b = 4 \rightarrow -3a + 4b + 2 =$

53) $x = -4, \ y = -3 \rightarrow 2x - 6 - 4y =$

Day 5: Answers

1) $2 - 3x - 1 \rightarrow 2 - 1 = 1 \rightarrow 2 - 3x - 1 = -3x + 1$

2) $-6 - 2x + 8 \rightarrow -6 + 8 = 2 \rightarrow -6 - 2x + 8 = -2x + 2$

3) $11x - 6x - 4 \rightarrow 11x - 6x = 5x \rightarrow 11x - 6x - 4 = 5x - 4$

4) $-16x + 25x - 5 \rightarrow -16x + 25x = 9x \rightarrow -16x + 25x - 5 = 9x - 5$

5) $5x + 5 - 15x \rightarrow 5x - 15x = -10x \rightarrow 5x + 5 - 15x = -10x + 5$

6) $4 + 5x - 6x - 5 \rightarrow 4 - 5 = -1, 5x - 6x = -x \rightarrow 4 + 5x - 6x - 5 = -x - 1$

7) $3x + 10 - 2x - 20 \rightarrow 10 - 20 = -10, 3x - 2x = x \rightarrow 3x + 10 - 2x - 20 = x - 10$

8) $-3 - 2x^2 - 5 + 3x \rightarrow -3 - 5 = -8 \rightarrow -3 - 2x^2 - 5 + 3x = -2x^2 + 3x - 8$

9) $-7 + 9x^2 - 2 + 2x \rightarrow -7 - 2 = -9 \rightarrow -7 + 9x^2 - 2 + 2x = 9x^2 + 2x - 9$

10) $4x^2 + 2x - 12x - 5 \rightarrow 2x - 12x = -10x \rightarrow 4x^2 + 2x - 12x - 5 = 4x^2 - 10x - 5$

11) $2x^2 - 3x - 5x + 6 - 9 \rightarrow -3x - 5x = -8x, 6 - 9 = -3 \rightarrow$

    $2x^2 - 3x - 5x + 6 - 9 = 2x^2 - 8x - 3$

12) $x^2 - 6x - x + 2 - 3 \rightarrow -6x - x = -7x, 2 - 3 = -1 \rightarrow x^2 - 6x - x + 2 - 3 = $
    $x^2 - 7x - 1$

13) $10x^2 - x - 8x + 3 - 10 \rightarrow -x - 8x = -9x, 3 - 10 = -7 \rightarrow 10x^2 - x - 8x + 3 - $
    $10 = 10x^2 - 9x - 7$

14) $4x^2 - 7x - x^2 + 2x + 5 \rightarrow 4x^2 - x^2 = 3x^2, -7x + 2x = -5x \rightarrow$

    $4x^2 - 7x - x^2 + 2x + 5 = 3x^2 - 5x + 5$

15) $4x^2 + 3x^3 - x^2 + x \rightarrow 4x^2 - x^2 = 3x^2 \rightarrow 4x^2 + 3x^3 - x^2 + x = 3x^3 + 3x^2 + x$

16) $5x^4 + x^5 - x^4 + 4x^2 \rightarrow 5x^4 - x^4 = 4x^4 \rightarrow 5x^4 + x^5 - x^4 + 4x^2 = $

    $4x^4 + x^5 + 4x^2 = x^5 + 4x^4 + 4x^2$

17) $15x^3 + 12x - 6x^2 - 9x^3 \rightarrow 15x^3 - 9x^3 = 6x^3 \rightarrow 15x^3 + 12x - 6x^2 - 9x^3 =$

   $6x^3 + 12x - 6x^2 = 6x^3 - 6x^2 + 12x$

18) $(7x^3 - 2x^2) + (6x^2 - 13x) = 7x^3 - 2x^2 + 6x^2 - 13x \rightarrow -2x^2 + 6x^2 = 4x^2 \rightarrow$
   $7x^3 - 2x^2 + 6x^2 - 13x = 7x^3 + 4x^2 - 13x$

19) $(9x^4 + 6x^3) + (11x^3 - 5x^4) = 9x^4 + 6x^3 + 11x^3 - 5x^4 \rightarrow 9x^4 - 5x^4 = 4x^4,$
   $6x^3 + 11x^3 = 17x^3 \rightarrow 9x^4 + 6x^3 + 11x^3 - 5x^4 = 4x^4 + 17x^3$

20) $(15x^5 - 5x^3) - (4x^3 + 6x^2) = 15x^5 - 5x^3 - 4x^3 - 6x^2 \rightarrow -5x^3 - 4x^3 = -9x^3 \rightarrow$
   $15x^5 - 5x^3 - 4x^3 - 6x^2 = 15x^5 - 9x^3 - 6x^2$

21) $(15x^4 + 7x^3) - (3x^3 - 26) = 15x^4 + 7x^3 - 3x^3 + 26 \rightarrow 7x^3 - 3x^3 = 4x^3 \rightarrow$
   $15x^4 + 7x^3 - 3x^3 + 26 = 15x^4 + 4x^3 + 26$

22) $(22x^4 + 6x^3) - (-2x^3 - 4x^4) = 22x^4 + 6x^3 + 2x^3 + 4x^4 \rightarrow 22x^4 + 4x^4 =$
   $26x^4, 6x^3 + 2x^3 = 8x^3 \rightarrow 22x^4 + 6x^3 + 2x^3 + 4x^4 = 26x^4 + 8x^3$

23) $(x^2 + 6x^3) + (-19x^2 + 6x^3) = x^2 + 6x^3 - 19x^2 + 6x^3 \rightarrow 6x^3 + 6x^3 = 12x^3,$
   $-19x^2 + x^2 = -18x^2 \rightarrow x^2 + 6x^3 - 19x^2 + 6x^3 = 12x^3 - 18x^2$

24) $(2x^4 - x^3) + (-5x^3 - 7x^4) = 2x^4 - x^3 - 5x^3 - 7x^4 \rightarrow 2x^4 - 7x^4 =$

   $-5x^4, -x^3 - 5x^3 = -6x^3 \rightarrow 2x^4 - x^3 - 5x^3 - 7x^4 = -5x^4 - 6x^3$

25) $3(5 + x) = (3) \times (5) + (3) \times x = 15 + 3x = 3x + 15$

26) $5(4 - x) = (5) \times (4) + (5) \times (-x) = 20 + (-5x) = -5x + 20$

27) $6(2 - 5x) = (6) \times (2) + (6) \times (-5x) = 12 + (-30x) = -30x + 12$

28) $(4 - 3x)7 = (4) \times (7) + (-3x) \times (7) = 28 + (-21x) = -21x + 28$

29) $8(3 - 3x) = (8) \times (3) + (8) \times (-3x) = 24 + (-24x) = -24x + 24$

30) $(-1)(-6 + 2x) = (-1) \times (-6) + (-1) \times (2x) = 6 + (-2x) = -2x + 6$

31) $(-5)(3x - 3) = (-5) \times (3x) + (-5) \times (-3) = -15x + 15$

32) $(-x + 10)(-3) = (-x) \times (-3) + (10) \times (-3) = 3x - 30$

33) $(-2)(2 - 6x) = (-2) \times (2) + (-2) \times (-6x) = -4 + 12x = 12x - 4$

34) $(-6x - 4)(-7) = (-6x) \times (-7) + (-4) \times (-7) = 42x + 28$

35) $x = 3 \rightarrow 12 - x = 12 - 3 = 9$

36) $x = 5 \rightarrow x + 7 = 5 + 7 = 12$

37) $x = 3 \rightarrow 3x - 5 = (3) \times (3) - 5 = 9 - 5 = 4$

38) $x = 2 \rightarrow 18 - 3x = 18 - (3) \times (2) = 18 - 6 = 12$

39) $x = 7 \rightarrow 5x - 4 = (5) \times (7) - 4 = 35 - 4 = 31$

40) $x = 6 \rightarrow 21 - x = 21 - 6 = 15$

41) $x = 5 \rightarrow 10x - 20 = (10) \times (5) - 20 = 50 - 20 = 30$

42) $x = -5 \rightarrow 4 - x = 4 - (-5) = 4 + 5 = 9$

43) $x = -2 \rightarrow 25 - 3x = 25 - (3) \times (-2) = 25 - (-6) = 25 + 6 = 31$

44) $x = -7 \rightarrow 16 - x = 16 - (-7) = 16 + 7 = 23$

45) $x = -13 \rightarrow 40 - 2x = 40 - (2) \times (-13) = 40 - (-26) = 40 + 26 = 66$

46) $x = -4 \rightarrow 20x - 6 = 20 \times (-4) - 6 = -80 - 6 = -86$

47) $x = -6 \rightarrow -11x - 19 = (-11) \times (-6) - 19 = 66 - 19 = 47$

48) $x = -8 \rightarrow -1 - 3x = (-1) - (3) \times (-8) = -1 - (-24) = -1 + 24 = 23$

49) $x = 3, \ y = 2 \rightarrow 3x + 2y = 3 \times (3) + 2(2) = 9 + 4 = 13$

50) $a = 4, \ b = 1 \rightarrow 2a - 6b = 2 \times (4) - 6(1) = 8 - 6 = 2$

51) $x = 5, \ y = 7 \rightarrow 2x - 4y - 5 = 2 \times (5) - 4(7) - 5 = 10 - 28 - 5 = -23$

52) $a = -3, \ b = 4 \rightarrow -3a + 4b + 2 = -3 \times (-3) + 4(4) + 2 = 9 + 16 + 2 = 27$

53) $x = -4, \ y = -3 \rightarrow 2x - 6 - 4y = 2 \times (-4) - 6 - 4(-3) = -8 - 6 + 12 = -2$

DAY 6

Equations and Inequalities

Math topics that you'll learn in this chapter:

1. One-Step Equations

2. Multi-Step Equations

3. System of Equations

4. Graphing Single–Variable Inequalities

5. One-Step Inequalities

6. Multi-Step Inequalities

69

One–Step Equations

☆ The values of two expressions on both sides of an equation are equal. Example: $ax = b$. In this equation, ax is equal to b.

☆ Solving an equation means finding the value of the variable.

☆ You only need to perform one Math operation to solve the one-step equations.

☆ To solve a one-step equation, find the inverse (opposite) operation is being performed.

☆ The inverse operations are:

  ❖ Addition and subtraction

  ❖ Multiplication and division

Examples:

Example 1. Solve this equation for x. $6x = 18 \rightarrow x = ?$

Solution: Here, the operation is multiplication (variable x is multiplied by 6) and its inverse operation is division. To solve this equation, divide both sides of equation by 6: $6x = 18 \rightarrow \frac{6x}{6} = \frac{18}{6} \rightarrow x = 3$

Example 2. Solve this equation. $x + 5 = 0 \rightarrow x = ?$

Solution: In this equation, 5 is added to the variable x. The inverse operation of addition is subtraction. To solve this equation, subtract 5 from both sides of the equation: $x + 5 - 5 = 0 - 5$. Then: $x + 5 - 5 = 0 - 5 \rightarrow x = -5$

Example 3. Solve this equation for x. $x - 11 = 0$

Solution: Here, the operation is subtraction and its inverse operation is addition. To solve this equation, add 11 to both sides of the equation: $x - 11 + 11 = 0 + 11 \rightarrow x = 11$

Multi–Step Equations

✩ To solve a multi-step equation, combine "like" terms on one side.

✩ Bring variables to one side by adding or subtracting.

✩ Simplify using the inverse of addition or subtraction.

✩ Simplify further by using the inverse of multiplication or division.

✩ Check your solution by plugging the value of the variable into the original equation.

Examples:

Example 1. Solve this equation for x. $5x - 6 = 26 - 3x$

Solution: First, bring variables to one side by adding $3x$ to both sides. Then:
$5x - 6 + 3x = 26 - 3x + 3x \rightarrow 5x - 6 + 3x = 26$.
Simplify: $8x - 6 = 26$. Now, add 6 to both sides of the equation:
$8x - 6 + 6 = 26 + 6 \rightarrow 8x = 32 \rightarrow$ Divide both sides by 8:
$8x = 32 \rightarrow \dfrac{8x}{8} = \dfrac{32}{8} \rightarrow x = 4$
Let's check this solution by substituting the value of 4 for x in the original equation:
$x = 4 \rightarrow 5x - 6 = 26 - 3x \rightarrow 5(4) - 6 = 26 - 3(4) \rightarrow 20 - 6 = 26 - 12 \rightarrow 14 = 14$
The answer $x = 4$ is correct.

Example 2. Solve this equation for x. $6x - 3 = 15$

Solution: Add 3 to both sides of the equation.
$6x - 3 = 15 \rightarrow 6x - 3 + 3 = 15 + 3 \rightarrow 6x = 18$
Divide both sides by 6, then: $6x = 18 \rightarrow \dfrac{6x}{6} = \dfrac{18}{6} \rightarrow x = 3$
Now, check the solution:
$x = 4 \rightarrow 6(3) - 3 = 15 \rightarrow 18 - 3 = 15 \rightarrow 15 = 15$
The answer $x = 4$ is correct.

System of Equations

☆ A system of equations contains two equations and two variables. For example, consider the system of equations: $x - y = 1$ and $x + y = 5$

☆ The easiest way to solve a system of equations is using the elimination method. The elimination method uses the addition property of equality. You can add the same value to each side of an equation.

☆ For the first equation above, you can add $x + y$ to the left side and 5 to the right side of the first equation: $x - y + (x + y) = 1 + 5$. Now, if you simplify, you get: $x - y + (x + y) = 1 + 5 \rightarrow 2x = 6 \rightarrow x = 3$. Now, substitute 3 for the x in the first equation: $3 - y = 1$. By solving this equation, $y = 2$

Example:

What is the value of $x + y$ in this system of equations?

$$\begin{cases} -x + y = 18 \\ 2x - 6y = -12 \end{cases}$$

Solution: Solving the system of equations by elimination:
Multiply the first equation by (2), then add it to the second equation.

$$\begin{array}{l} 2(-x + y = 18) \\ \underline{2x - 6y = -12} \end{array} \Rightarrow \begin{array}{l} -2x + 2y = 36 \\ 2x - 6y = -12 \end{array} \Rightarrow (-2x) + 2x + 2y - 6y = 36 - 12 \Rightarrow -4y = 24 \Rightarrow$$

$y = -6$

Plug in the value of y into one of the equations and solve for x.
$-x + (-6) = 18 \Rightarrow -x - 6 = 18 \Rightarrow -x = 24 \Rightarrow x = -24$
Thus, $x + y = -24 - 6 = -30$

Graphing Single–Variable Inequalities

☆ An inequality compares two expressions using an inequality sign.

☆ Inequality signs are: "less than" <, "greater than" >, "less than or equal to" ≤, and "greater than or equal to" ≥.

☆ To graph a single–variable inequality, find the value of the inequality on the number line.

☆ For less than (<) or greater than (>) draw an open circle on the value of the variable. If there is an equal sign too, then use a filled circle.

☆ Draw an arrow to the right for greater or to the left for less than.

Examples:

Draw a graph for this inequality. $x > 3$

Solution: Since the variable is greater than 3, then we need to find 3 in the number line and draw an open circle on it. Then, draw an arrow to the right.

Examp   Graph this inequality. $x \leq -1$.

Solution: Since the variable is less than or equal to −1, then we need to find −1 on the number line and draw a filled circle on it. Then, draw an arrow to the left.

One–Step Inequalities

☆ An inequality compares two expressions using an inequality sign.

☆ Inequality signs are: "less than" <, "greater than" >, "less than or equal to" ≤, and "greater than or equal to" ≥.

☆ You only need to perform one Math operation to solve the one-step inequalities.

☆ To solve one-step inequalities, find the inverse (opposite) operation is being performed.

☆ For dividing or multiplying both sides by negative numbers, flip the direction of the inequality sign.

Examples:

Example 1. Solve this inequality for x. $x + 7 \geq 2$

Solution: The inverse (opposite) operation of addition is subtraction. In this inequality, 7 is added to x. To isolate x we need to subtract 7 from both sides of the inequality.
Then: $x + 7 \geq 2 \to x + 7 - 7 \geq 2 - 7 \to x \geq -5$. The solution is: $x \geq -5$

Example 2. Solve the inequality. $x - 2 > -12$

Solution: 2 is subtracted from x. Add 2 to both sides.
$x - 2 > -12 \to x - 2 + 2 > -12 + 2 \to x > -10$

Example 3. Solve. $6x \leq -36$

Solution: 6 is multiplied to x. Divide both sides by 6.
Then: $6x \leq -36 \to \frac{6x}{6} \leq \frac{-36}{6} \to x \leq -6$

Example 4. Solve. $-2x \leq 10$

Solution: -2 is multiplied to x. Divide both sides by -2. Remember when dividing or multiplying both sides of an inequality by negative numbers, flip the direction of the inequality sign.
Then: $-2x \leq 10 \to \frac{-2x}{-2} \geq \frac{10}{-2} \to x \geq -5$

Multi–Step Inequalities

✫ To solve a multi-step inequality, combine "like" terms on one side.

✫ Bring variables to one side by adding or subtracting.

✫ Isolate the variable.

✫ Simplify using the inverse of addition or subtraction.

✫ Simplify further by using the inverse of multiplication or division.

✫ For dividing or multiplying both sides by negative numbers, flip the direction of the inequality sign.

Examples:

Example 1. Solve this inequality. $4x - 1 \leq 23$

Solution: In this inequality, 1 is subtracted from $4x$. The inverse of subtraction is addition. Add 1 to both sides of the inequality:

$4x - 1 + 1 \leq 23 + 1 \rightarrow 4x \leq 24$

Now, divide both sides by 4. Then: $4x \leq 24 \rightarrow \frac{4x}{4} \leq \frac{24}{4} \rightarrow x \leq 6$

The solution of this inequality is $x \leq 6$.

Example 2. Solve this inequality. $2x - 6 < 18$

Solution: First, add 6 to both sides: $2x - 6 + 6 < 18 + 6$

Then simplify: $2x - 6 + 6 < 18 + 6 \rightarrow 2x < 24$

Now divide both sides by 2: $\frac{2x}{2} < \frac{24}{2} \rightarrow x < 12$

Example 3. Solve this inequality. $-4x - 8 \geq 12$

Solution: First, add 8 to both sides:

$-4x - 8 + 8 \geq 12 + 8 \rightarrow -4x \geq 20$

Divide both sides by -4. Remember that you need to flip the direction of inequality sign. $-4x \geq 20 \rightarrow \frac{-4x}{-4} \leq \frac{20}{-4} \rightarrow x \leq -5$

Day 6: Practices

✍ Solve each equation. (One–Step Equations)

1) $x + 2 = 5 \rightarrow x =$

2) $8 = 13 + x \rightarrow x =$

3) $-6 = 7 + x \rightarrow x =$

4) $x - 5 = -3 \rightarrow x =$

5) $-13 = x - 15 \rightarrow x =$

6) $-10 + x = -4 \rightarrow x =$

7) $-19 + x = 7 \rightarrow x =$

8) $-6x = 24 \rightarrow x =$

9) $\frac{x}{4} = -5 \rightarrow x =$

10) $-2x = -4 \rightarrow x =$

✍ Solve each equation. (Multi–Step Equations)

11) $2(x + 5) = 16 \rightarrow x =$

12) $-6(3 - x) = 18 \rightarrow x =$

13) $25 = -5(x + 4) \rightarrow x =$

14) $-12 = 6(9 + x) \rightarrow x =$

15) $11(x + 5) = -22 \rightarrow x =$

16) $-27 - 36x = 45 \rightarrow x =$

17) $3x - 4 = x - 12 \rightarrow x =$

18) $-8x + x - 11 = 24 \rightarrow x =$

✍ Solve each system of equations.

19) $\begin{cases} x + 4y = 29 \\ x + 2y = 5 \end{cases}$ $x = \underline{\quad}$ $y = \underline{\quad}$

21) $\begin{cases} 2x + 5y = 15 \\ x + y = 6 \end{cases}$ $x = \underline{\quad}$ $y = \underline{\quad}$

20) $\begin{cases} 2x + y = 36 \\ x + 4y = 4 \end{cases}$ $x = \underline{\quad}$ $y = \underline{\quad}$

22) $\begin{cases} 2x - 2y = -16 \\ -9x + 2y = -19 \end{cases}$ $x = \underline{\quad}$ $y = \underline{\quad}$

✍ Draw a graph for each inequality.

23) $x \leq 1$

24) $x > -4$

✍ Solve each inequality and graph it.

25) $x - 3 \geq -2$

26) $7x - 6 < 8$

✍ Solve each inequality.

27) $x + 11 > 3$

28) $x + 4 > 1$

29) $-6 + 3x \leq 21$

30) $-5 + 4x \leq 19$

31) $4 + 9x \leq 31$

32) $8(x + 3) \geq -16$

33) $3(6 + x) \geq 18$

34) $3(x - 2) < -9$

35) $15 + 9x < -30$

36) $3(6 - x) \geq -27$

37) $4(x - 5) \geq -32$

38) $6(x + 4) < -24$

39) $7(x - 8) \geq -49$

40) $-(-6 - 5x) > -39$

41) $2(1 - 2x) > -66$

42) $-3(3 - 2x) > -33$

Day 6: Answers

1) $x + 2 = 5 \rightarrow x = 5 - 2 = 3$

2) $8 = 13 + x \rightarrow x = 8 - 13 = -5$

3) $-6 = 7 + x \rightarrow x = -6 - 7 = -13$

4) $x - 5 = -3 \rightarrow x = -3 + 5 = 2$

5) $-13 = x - 15 \rightarrow x = -13 + 15 = 2$

6) $-10 + x = -4 \rightarrow x = -4 + 10 = 6$

7) $-19 + x = 7 \rightarrow x = 7 + 19 = 26$

8) $-6x = 24 \rightarrow x = \frac{24}{-6} = -4$

9) $\frac{x}{4} = -5 \rightarrow x = -5 \times 4 = -20$

10) $-2x = -4 \rightarrow x = \frac{-4}{-2} = 2$

11) $2(x + 5) = 16 \rightarrow \frac{2(x+5)}{2} = \frac{16}{2} \rightarrow (x + 5) = 8 \rightarrow x = 8 - 5 = 3$

12) $-6(3 - x) = 18 \rightarrow \frac{-6(3-x)}{-6} = \frac{18}{-6} \rightarrow (3 - x) = -3 \rightarrow x = 3 + 3 = 6$

13) $25 = -5(x + 4) \rightarrow \frac{25}{-5} = \frac{-5(x+4)}{-5} \rightarrow -5 = (x + 4) \rightarrow x = -5 - 4 = -9$

14) $-12 = 6(9 + x) \rightarrow \frac{-12}{6} = \frac{6(9+x)}{6} \rightarrow -2 = (9 + x) \rightarrow x = -2 - 9 = -11$

15) $11(x + 5) = -22 \rightarrow \frac{11(x+5)}{11} = \frac{-22}{11} \rightarrow (x + 5) = -2 \rightarrow x = -2 - 5 = -7$

16) $-27 - 36x = 45 \rightarrow -36x = 45 + 27 \rightarrow -36x = 72 \rightarrow \frac{-36x}{-2} = \frac{72}{-2} \rightarrow x = -2$

17) $3x - 4 = x - 12 \rightarrow 3x - 4 - x = x - 12 - x \rightarrow 2x - 4 = -12 \rightarrow 2x = -12 + 4 \rightarrow$

$2x = -8 \rightarrow \frac{2x}{2} = \frac{-8}{2} \rightarrow x = -4$

18) $-8x + x - 11 = 24 \rightarrow -7x = 24 + 11 \rightarrow \frac{-7x}{-7} = \frac{35}{-7} \rightarrow x = -5$

19) $\begin{cases} x + 4y = 29 \\ x + 2y = 5 \end{cases} \rightarrow \begin{array}{c} -(x + 4y = 29) \\ x + 2y = 5 \end{array} \rightarrow \begin{array}{c} -x - 4y = -29 \\ x + 2y = 5 \end{array} \rightarrow (-x) + x - 4y + 2y =$

$-29 + 5 \rightarrow -2y = -24 \rightarrow \frac{-2y}{-2} = \frac{-24}{-2} \rightarrow y = 12$

Plug in the value of y into one of the equations and solve for x.
$x + 2y = 5 \rightarrow x + 2(12) = 5 \rightarrow x + 24 = 5 \rightarrow x = 5 - 24 = -19$

20) $\begin{cases} 2x + y = 36 \\ x + 4y = 4 \end{cases} \rightarrow \begin{matrix} 2x + y = 36 \\ -2(x + 4y = 4) \end{matrix} \rightarrow \begin{matrix} 2x + y = 36 \\ -2x - 8y = -8 \end{matrix} \rightarrow 2x - 2x + y - 8y = 36 -$

$8 \rightarrow -7y = 28 \rightarrow \frac{-7y}{-7} = \frac{28}{-7} \rightarrow y = -4$

Plug in the value of y into one of the equations and solve for x.

$x + 4y = 4 \rightarrow x + 4(-4) = 4 \rightarrow x - 16 = 4 \rightarrow x = 4 + 16 = 20$

21) $\begin{cases} 2x + 5y = 15 \\ x + y = 6 \end{cases} \rightarrow \begin{matrix} 2x + 5y = 15 \\ -2(x + y = 6) \end{matrix} \rightarrow \begin{matrix} 2x + 5y = 15 \\ -2x - 2y = -12 \end{matrix} \rightarrow 2x - 2x + 5y - 2y = 15 -$

$12 \rightarrow 3y = 3 \rightarrow \frac{3y}{3} = \frac{3}{3} \rightarrow y = 1$

Plug in the value of y into one of the equations and solve for x.

$x + y = 6 \rightarrow x + 1 = 6 \rightarrow x = 6 - 1 = 5$

22) $\begin{cases} 2x - 2y = -16 \\ -9x + 2y = -19 \end{cases} \rightarrow 2x - 9x - 2y + 2y = -16 - 19 \rightarrow -7x = -35 \rightarrow \frac{-7x}{-7} =$

$\frac{-35}{-7} \rightarrow x = 5$

Plug in the value of x into one of the equations and solve for y.

$2x - 2y = -16 \rightarrow 2(5) - 2y = -16 \rightarrow 10 - 2y = -16 \rightarrow 10 + 16 = 2y \rightarrow 26 = 2y$

$\rightarrow \frac{26}{2} = \frac{2y}{2} \rightarrow y = 13$

23) $x \le 1$

24) $x > -4$

25) $x - 3 \ge -2 \rightarrow x \ge -2 + 3 \rightarrow x \ge 1$

26) $7x - 6 < 8 \rightarrow 7x < 8 + 6 \rightarrow 7x < 14 \rightarrow x < \frac{14 \div 7}{7 \div 7} \rightarrow x < 2$

27) $x + 11 > 3 \rightarrow x > 3 - 11 \rightarrow x > -8$

28) $x + 4 > 1 \rightarrow x > 1 - 4 \rightarrow x > -3$

29) $-6 + 3x \le 21 \rightarrow 3x \le 21 + 6 \rightarrow 3x \le 27 \rightarrow x \le \frac{27 \div 3}{3 \div 3} \rightarrow x \le 9$

30) $-5 + 4x \le 19 \rightarrow 4x \le 19 + 5 \rightarrow 4x \le 24 \rightarrow x \le \frac{24 \div 4}{4 \div 4} \rightarrow x \le 6$

31) $4 + 9x \leq 31 \rightarrow 9x \leq 31 - 4 \rightarrow 9x \leq 27 \rightarrow x \leq \frac{27 \div 9}{9 \div 9} \rightarrow x \leq 3$

32) $8(x + 3) \geq -16 \rightarrow x + 3 \geq \frac{-16}{8} \rightarrow x + 3 \geq -2 \rightarrow x \geq -2 - 3 \rightarrow x \geq -5$

33) $3(6 + x) \geq 18 \rightarrow 6 + x \geq \frac{18}{3} \rightarrow 6 + x \geq 6 \rightarrow x \geq 6 - 6 \rightarrow x \geq 0$

34) $3(x - 2) < -9 \rightarrow x - 2 < \frac{-9}{3} \rightarrow x - 2 < -3 \rightarrow x < -3 + 2 \rightarrow x < -1$

35) $15 + 9x < -30 \rightarrow 9x < -30 - 15 \rightarrow 9x < -45 \rightarrow x < \frac{-45}{9} \rightarrow x < -5$

36) $3(6 - x) \geq -27 \rightarrow 6 - x \geq \frac{-27}{3} \rightarrow 6 - x \geq -9 \rightarrow -x \geq -9 - 6 \rightarrow \frac{-x}{-1} \leq \frac{-15}{-1} \rightarrow$

$x \leq 15$

37) $4(x - 5) \geq -32 \rightarrow x - 5 \geq \frac{-32}{4} \rightarrow x - 5 \geq -8 \rightarrow x \geq -8 + 5 \rightarrow x \geq -3$

38) $6(x + 4) < -24 \rightarrow x + 4 < \frac{-24}{6} \rightarrow x + 4 < -4 \rightarrow x < -4 - 4 \rightarrow x < -8$

39) $7(x - 8) \geq -49 \rightarrow x - 8 \geq \frac{-49}{7} \rightarrow x - 8 \geq -7 \rightarrow x \geq -7 + 8 \rightarrow x \geq 1$

40) $-(-6 - 5x) > -39 \rightarrow 6 + 5x > -39 \rightarrow 5x > -39 - 6 \rightarrow 5x > -45 \rightarrow$

$x > \frac{-45}{5} \rightarrow x > -9$

41) $2(1 - 2x) > -66 \rightarrow 1 - 2x > \frac{-66}{2} \rightarrow 1 - 2x > -33 \rightarrow -2x > -33 - 1 \rightarrow$

$-2x > -34 \rightarrow x < \frac{-34}{-2} \rightarrow x < \frac{-34}{-2} \rightarrow x < 17$

42) $-3(3 - 2x) > -33 \rightarrow -9 + 6x > -33 \rightarrow 6x > -33 + 9 \rightarrow 6x > -24 \rightarrow$

$\frac{6x}{6} > \frac{-24}{6} \rightarrow x > -4$

Lines and Slope

Math topics that you'll learn in this chapter:

1. Finding Slope
2. Graphing Lines Using Slope–Intercept Form
3. Writing Linear Equations
4. Finding Midpoint
5. Finding Distance of Two Points
6. Graphing Linear Inequalities

81

Finding Slope

✰ The slope of a line represents the direction of a line on the coordinate plane.

✰ A coordinate plane contains two perpendicular number lines. The horizontal line is x and the vertical line is y. The point at which the two axes intersect is called the origin. An ordered pair (x, y) shows the location of a point.

✰ A line on a coordinate plane can be drawn by connecting two points.

✰ To find the slope of a line, we need the equation of the line or two points on the line.

✰ The slope of a line with two points A (x_1, y_1) and B (x_2, y_2) can be found by using this formula: $\frac{y_2 - y_1}{x_2 - x_1} = \frac{rise}{run}$

✰ The equation of a line is typically written as $y = mx + b$ where m is the slope and b is the y-intercept.

Examples:

Example 1. Find the slope of the line through these two points:

A$(5, -5)$ and $B(9, 7)$.

Solution: Slope $= \frac{y_2 - y_1}{x_2 - x_1}$. Let (x_1, y_1) be A$(5, -5)$ and (x_2, y_2) be $B(9, 7)$.

(Remember, you can choose any point for (x_1, y_1) and (x_2, y_2)).

Then: slope $= \frac{y_2 - y_1}{x_2 - x_1} = \frac{7 - (-5)}{9 - 5} = \frac{12}{4} = 3$

The slope of the line through these two points is 3.

Example 2. Find the slope of the line with equation $y = -2x + 8$

Solution: When the equation of a line is written in the form of $y = mx + b$, the slope is m. In this line: $y = -2x + 8$, the slope is -2.

Graphing Lines Using Slope–Intercept Form

☆ Slope–intercept form of a line: given the slope m and the y–intercept (the intersection of the line and y-axis) b, then the equation of the line is:

$$y = mx + b$$

☆ To draw the graph of a linear equation in a slope-intercept form on the xy coordinate plane, find two points on the line by plugging two values for x and calculating the values of y.

☆ You can also use the slope (m) and one point to graph the line.

Example:

Sketch the graph of $y = -3x + 6$.

Solution: To graph this line, we need to find two points. When x is zero the value of y is 6. And when y is 0 the value of x is 2.

$$x = 0 \rightarrow y = -3(0) + 6 = 6$$
$$y = 0 \rightarrow 0 = -3x + 6 \rightarrow x = 2$$

Now, we have two points:
$(0, 6)$ and $(2, 0)$.
Find the points on the coordinate plane and graph the line. Remember that the slope of the line is -3.

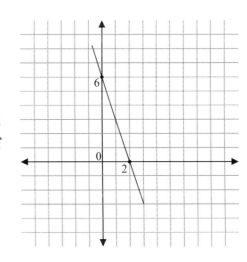

Writing Linear Equations

✩ The equation of a line in slope-intercept form: $y = mx + b$

✩ To write the equation of a line, first identify the slope.

✩ Find the y-intercept. This can be done by substituting the slope and the coordinates of a point (x, y) on the line.

Examples:

Example 1. What is the equation of the line that passes through $(-7, 2)$ and has a slope of 4?

Solution: The general slope-intercept form of the equation of a line is $y = mx + b$, where m is the slope and b is the y-intercept.

By substitution of the given point and given slope:

$y = mx + b \rightarrow 2 = (4)(-7) + b$. So, $b = 2 + 28 = 30$, and the required equation of the line is: $y = 4x + 30$

Example 2. Write the equation of the line through two points $A(5, 2)$ and $B(3, -4)$.

Solution: First, find the slope: $Slop = \frac{y_2 - y_1}{x_2 - x_1} = \frac{-4 - 2}{3 - 5} = \frac{-6}{-2} = 3 \rightarrow m = 3$

To find the value of b, use either points and plug in the values of x and y in the equation. The answer will be the same: $y = x + b$. Let's check both points. Then:

$(5, 2) \rightarrow y = mx + b \rightarrow 2 = 3(5) + b \rightarrow b = -13$

$(3, -4) \rightarrow y = mx + b \rightarrow -4 = 3(3) + b \rightarrow b = -13$.

The y-intercept of the line is -13. The equation of the line is: $y = 3x - 13$

Example 3. What is the equation of the line that passes through $(3, -4)$ and has a slope of 2?

Solution: The general slope-intercept form of the equation of a line is $y = mx + b$, where m is the slope and b is the y-intercept. By substitution of the given point and given slope: $y = mx + b \rightarrow -4 = (2)(3) + b$

So, $b = -4 - 6 = -10$, and the equation of the line is: $y = 2x - 10$.

Finding Midpoint

✰ The middle of a line segment is its midpoint.

✰ The Midpoint of two endpoints A (x_1, y_1) and B (x_2, y_2) can be found using this formula: $M = \left(\frac{x_1+x_2}{2}, \frac{y_1+y_2}{2}\right)$

Examples:

Example 1. Find the midpoint of the line segment with the given endpoints. $(3, 5), (1, 3)$

Solution: Midpoint $= \left(\frac{x_1+x_2}{2}, \frac{y_1+y_2}{2}\right) \rightarrow (x_1, y_1) = (3, 5)$ and $(x_2, y_2) = (1, 3)$
Midpoint $= \left(\frac{3+1}{2}, \frac{5+3}{2}\right) \rightarrow \left(\frac{4}{2}, \frac{8}{2}\right) \rightarrow M(2, 4)$

Example 2. Find the midpoint of the line segment with the given endpoints. $(-1, 3), (9, -9)$

Solution: Midpoint $= \left(\frac{x_1+x_2}{2}, \frac{y_1+y_2}{2}\right) \rightarrow (x_1, y_1) = (-1, 3)$ and $(x_2, y_2) = (9, -9)$
Midpoint $= \left(\frac{-1+9}{2}, \frac{3+(-9)}{2}\right) \rightarrow \left(\frac{8}{2}, \frac{-6}{2}\right) \rightarrow M(4, -3)$

Example 3. Find the midpoint of the line segment with the given endpoints. $(8, 4), (-2, 6)$

Solution: Midpoint $= \left(\frac{x_1+x_2}{2}, \frac{y_1+y_2}{2}\right) \rightarrow (x_1, y_1) = (8, 4)$ and $(x_2, y_2) = (-2, 6)$
Midpoint $= \left(\frac{8-2}{2}, \frac{4+6}{2}\right) \rightarrow \left(\frac{6}{2}, \frac{10}{2}\right) \rightarrow M(3, 5)$

Example 4. Find the midpoint of the line segment with the given endpoints. $(7, -4), (-3, -8)$

Solution: Midpoint $= \left(\frac{x_1+x_2}{2}, \frac{y_1+y_2}{2}\right) \rightarrow (x_1, y_1) = (7, -4)$ and $(x_2, y_2) = (-3, -8)$
Midpoint $= \left(\frac{7-3}{2}, \frac{-4-8}{2}\right) \rightarrow \left(\frac{4}{2}, \frac{-12}{2}\right) \rightarrow M(2, -6)$

Finding Distance of Two Points

☆ Use the following formula to find the distance of two points with the coordinates A (x_1, y_1) and B (x_2, y_2):

$$d = \sqrt{(x_2 - x_1)^2 + (y_2 - y_1)^2}$$

Examples:

Example 1. Find the distance between $(5, -6)$ and $(-3, 9)$. on the coordinate plane.

Solution: Use distance of two points formula: $d = \sqrt{(x_2 - x_1)^2 + (y_2 - y_1)^2}$

$(x_1, y_1) = (5, -6)$ and $(x_2, y_2) = (-3, 9)$. Then: $d = \sqrt{(x_2 - x_1)^2 + (y_2 - y_1)^2} =$

$\sqrt{(-3 - 5)^2 + (9 - (-6))^2} = \sqrt{(-8)^2 + (15)^2} = \sqrt{64 + 225} = \sqrt{289} = 17.$

Then: $d = 17$

Example 2. Find the distance of two points $(-3, 10)$ and $(-9, 2)$

Solution: Use distance of two points formula: $d = \sqrt{(x_2 - x_1)^2 + (y_2 - y_1)^2}$

$(x_1, y_1) = (-3, 10)$ and $(x_2, y_2) = (-9, 2)$

Then: $d = \sqrt{(x_2 - x_1)^2 + (y_2 - y_1)^2} \rightarrow d = \sqrt{(-9 - (-3))^2 + (2 - 10)^2} =$

$\sqrt{(-6)^2 + (-8)^2} = \sqrt{36 + 64} = \sqrt{100} = 10.$ Then: $d = 10$

Example 3. Find the distance between $(-8, 7)$ and $(4, -9)$.

Solution: Use distance of two points formula: $d = \sqrt{(x_2 - x_1)^2 + (y_2 - y_1)^2}$

$(x_1, y_1) = (-8, 7)$ and $(x_2, y_2) = (4, -9)$. Then: $d = \sqrt{(x_2 - x_1)^2 + (y_2 - y_1)^2}$

$d = \sqrt{(4 - (-8))^2 + (-9 - 7)^2} = \sqrt{(12)^2 + (-16)^2} = \sqrt{144 + 256} = \sqrt{400} = 20.$

Then: $d = 20$

Graphing Linear Inequalities

✫ To graph a linear inequality, first draw a graph of the "equals" line.

✫ Use a dash line for less than ($<$) and greater than ($>$) signs and a solid line for less than and equal to ($\leq$) and greater than and equal to ($\geq$).

✫ Choose a testing point. (it can be any point on both sides of the line.)

✫ Put the value of (x, y) of that point in the inequality. If that works, that part of the line is the solution. If the values don't work, then the other part of the line is the solution.

Example:

Sketch the graph of inequality: $y > 2x - 5$

Solution: To draw the graph of $y > 2x - 5$, you first need to graph the line:

$y = 2x - 5$

Since there is a greater than ($>$) sign, draw a dash line.

The slope is 2 and y-intercept is -5.

Then, choose a testing point and substitute the value of x and y from that point into the inequality. The easiest point to test is the origin: $(0, 0)$

$(0, 0) \to y > 2x - 5 \to 0 > 2(0) - 5 \to 0 > -5$

This is correct! 0 is greater than -5. So, this part of the line (on the left side) is the solution of this inequality.

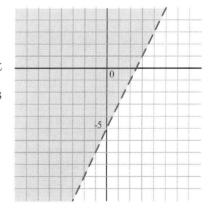

Day 7: Practices

✎ Find the slope of each line.

1) $y = x - 3$

2) $y = 3x + 4$

3) $y = -2x + 4$

4) Line through $(2, 5)$ and $(3, -4)$

5) Line through $(0, 6)$ and $(2, 4)$

6) Line through $(-2, 4)$ and $(3, -6)$

✎ Sketch the graph of each line. (Using Slope–Intercept Form)

7) $y = x + 3$

8) $y = x - 3$

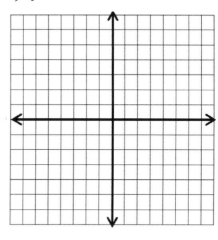

✎ Solve.

9) What is the equation of a line with slope 3 and intercept 12?

   _____

10) What is the equation of a line with slope 4 and passes through point

   $(2, 4)$? _____

11) What is the equation of a line with slope -2 and passes through point $(5, -3)$?

   _____

12) The slope of a line is -5 and it passes through point$(-4, 3)$. What is the

   equation of the line? _____

13) The slope of a line is -6 and it passes through point$(-2, -3)$. What is

   the equation of the line? _____

✎ Sketch the graph of each linear inequality.

14) $y > 3x - 3$

15) $y > -2x + 1$

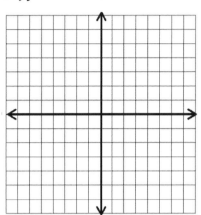

✎ Find the midpoint of the line segment with the given endpoints.

16) $(4, 1), (2, 3)$

17) $(3, 6), (5, 4)$

18) $(7, 1), (1, 3)$

19) $(2, 8), (2, 10)$

20) $(3, -2), (-1, 6)$

21) $(-1, -3), (1, 5)$

22) $(1, 4), (-7, 6)$

23) $(-3, 5), (7, -9)$

✎ Find the distance between each pair of points.

24) $(-8, -1), (-4, 2)$

25) $(-15, 2), (5, -13)$

26) $(-1, 11), (-7, 3)$

27) $(0, 11), (9, 11)$

28) $(-2, 4), (3, -8)$

29) $(6, -7), (-9, 1)$

30) $(8, -4), (-4, -20)$

31) $(5, 1), (9, -2)$

32) $(-8, -17), (2, 7)$

33) $(18, 21), (-12, 5)$

Day 7: Answers

1) $y = mx + b$, the slope is m. In this line: $y = x - 3$, the slope is $m = 1$.

2) $y = 3x + 4$, the slope is $m = 3$.

3) $y = -2x + 4$, the slope is $m = -2$.

4) $(x_1, y_1) = (2, 5)$ and $(x_2, y_2) = (3, 4) \rightarrow m = \frac{y_2 - y_1}{x_2 - x_1} = \frac{4-5}{3-2} = \frac{-1}{1} = -1$

5) $(x_1, y_1) = (0, 6)$ and $(x_2, y_2) = (2, -4) \rightarrow m = \frac{y_2 - y_1}{x_2 - x_1} = \frac{-4-6}{2-0} = \frac{-10}{2} = -5$

6) $(x_1, y_1) = (-2, 4)$ and $(x_2, y_2) = (3, -6) \rightarrow m = \frac{y_2 - y_1}{x_2 - x_1} = \frac{-6-4}{3-(-2)} = \frac{-6-4}{3+2} = \frac{-10}{5} = -2$

7) $y = x + 3$

$x = 0 \rightarrow y = 0 + 3 = 3 \rightarrow (0, 3)$

$y = 0 \rightarrow 0 = x + 3 \rightarrow x = -3$

$\rightarrow (-3, 0)$

$x = 1 \rightarrow y = 1 + 3 = 4 \rightarrow (1, 4)$

$y = 1 \rightarrow 1 = x + 3 \rightarrow x = 1 - 3$

$= -2 \rightarrow (-2, 1)$

8) $y = x - 3$

$x = 0 \rightarrow y = 0 - 3 = -3 \rightarrow (0, -3)$

$y = 0 \rightarrow 0 = x - 3 \rightarrow x = 3 \rightarrow$

$\rightarrow (3, 0)$

$x = 1 \rightarrow y = 1 - 3 = -2 \rightarrow (1, -2)$

$y = 1 \rightarrow 1 = x - 3 \rightarrow x = 1 + 3 = 4$

$\rightarrow (4, 1)$

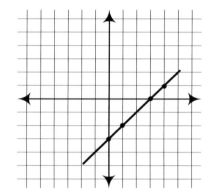

9) The general slope-intercept form of the equation of a line is $y = mx + b$, where m is the slope and b is the y-intercept $\rightarrow y = 3x + 12$

10) $y = mx + b \rightarrow 4 = 4(2) + b \rightarrow 4 = 8 + b \rightarrow b = 4 - 8 = -4 \rightarrow y = 4x - 4$

11) $y = mx + b \rightarrow -3 = -2(5) + b \rightarrow -3 = -10 + b \rightarrow b = -3 + 10 = 7 \rightarrow y = -2x + 7$

12) $y = mx + b \rightarrow 3 = -5(-4) + b \rightarrow 3 = 20 + b \rightarrow b = 3 - 20 = -17 \rightarrow y = -5x - 17$

13) $y = mx + b \rightarrow -3 = -6(-2) + b \rightarrow -3 = 12 + b \rightarrow b = -3 - 12 = -15 \rightarrow y = -6x - 15$

14) $y > 3x - 3$

$x = 0 \rightarrow y = 0 - 3 = -3 \rightarrow (0, -3)$

$y = 0 \to 0 = 3x - 3 \to 3x = 3 \to x = 1 \to (1, 0)$

The easiest point to test is the origin: $(0, 0)$

$(0,0) \to y > 3x - 3 \to 0 > 3(0) - 3 \to 0 > -3$

This is correct! 0 is greater than -3. So, this part of the line (on the left side) is the solution of this inequality.

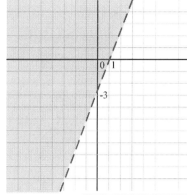

15) $y > -2x + 1$

$x = 0 \to y = 0 + 1 = 1 \to (0, 1)$

$y = 0 \to 0 = -2x + 1 \to -2x = -1 \to x = \dfrac{-1}{-2}$

$= 0.5 \to (0.5, 0)$

The easiest point to test is the origin: $(0, 0)$

$(0,0) \to y > -2x + 1 \to 0 > -2(0) + 1 \to 0 > 1$

This is incorrect! 0 is less than 1. So, this part of the line (on the right side) is the solution of this inequality.

16) $M = \left(\frac{x_1 + x_2}{2}, \frac{y_1 + y_2}{2}\right) \to (x_1, y_1) = (4, 1)$ and $(x_2, y_2) = (2, 3) \to M = \left(\frac{4+2}{2}, \frac{1+3}{2}\right) \to$ $\left(\frac{6}{2}, \frac{4}{2}\right) \to M(3, 2)$

17) $(x_1, y_1) = (3, 6)$ and $(x_2, y_2) = (5, 4) \to M = \left(\frac{3+5}{2}, \frac{6+4}{2}\right) \to \left(\frac{8}{2}, \frac{10}{2}\right) \to M(4, 5)$

18) $(x_1, y_1) = (7, 1)$ and $(x_2, y_2) = (1, 3) \to M = \left(\frac{7+1}{2}, \frac{1+3}{2}\right) \to \left(\frac{8}{2}, \frac{4}{2}\right) \to M(4, 2)$

19) $(x_1, y_1) = (2, 8)$ and $(x_2, y_2) = (2, 10) \to M = \left(\frac{2+2}{2}, \frac{8+10}{2}\right) \to \left(\frac{4}{2}, \frac{18}{2}\right) \to M(2, 9)$

20) $(x_1, y_1) = (3, -2)$ and $(x_2, y_2) = (-1, 6) \to M = \left(\frac{3-1}{2}, \frac{-2+6}{2}\right) \to \left(\frac{2}{2}, \frac{4}{2}\right) \to M(1, 2)$

21) $(x_1, y_1) = (-1, -3)$ and $(x_2, y_2) = (1, 5) \to M = \left(\frac{-1+1}{2}, \frac{-3+5}{2}\right) \to \left(\frac{0}{2}, \frac{2}{2}\right) \to M(0, 1)$

22) $(x_1, y_1) = (1, 4)$ and $(x_2, y_2) = (-7, 6) \to M = \left(\frac{1-7}{2}, \frac{4+6}{2}\right) \to \left(\frac{-6}{2}, \frac{10}{2}\right) \to M(-3, 5)$

23) $(x_1, y_1) = (-3, 5)$ and $(x_2, y_2) = (7, -9) \to M = \left(\frac{-3+7}{2}, \frac{5-9}{2}\right) \to \left(\frac{4}{2}, \frac{-4}{2}\right) \to M(2, -2)$

24) $(x_1, y_1) = (-8, -1)$ and $(x_2, y_2) = (-4, 2) \to d = \sqrt{(x_2 - x_1)^2 + (y_2 - y_1)^2} =$ $\sqrt{(-4 - (-8))^2 + (2 - (-1))^2} = \sqrt{(4)^2 + (3)^2} = \sqrt{16 + 9} = \sqrt{25} = 5$

25) $(x_1, y_1) = (-15, 2)$ and $(x_2, y_2) = (5, -13) \rightarrow d = \sqrt{(x_2 - x_1)^2 + (y_2 - y_1)^2} = $
$\sqrt{(5 - (-15))^2 + (-13 - 2)^2} = \sqrt{(20)^2 + (-15)^2} = \sqrt{400 + 225} = \sqrt{625} = 25$

26) $(x_1, y_1) = (-1, 11)$ and $(x_2, y_2) = (-7, 3) \rightarrow d = \sqrt{(x_2 - x_1)^2 + (y_2 - y_1)^2} = $
$\sqrt{(-7 - (-1))^2 + (3 - 11)^2} = \sqrt{(-6)^2 + (-8)^2} = \sqrt{36 + 64} = \sqrt{100} = 10$

27) $(x_1, y_1) = (0, 11)$ and $(x_2, y_2) = (9, 11) \rightarrow d = \sqrt{(x_2 - x_1)^2 + (y_2 - y_1)^2} = $
$\sqrt{(9 - 0)^2 + (11 - 11)^2} = \sqrt{(9)^2 + (0)^2} = \sqrt{81} = 9$

28) $(x_1, y_1) = (-2, 4)$ and $(x_2, y_2) = (3, -8) \rightarrow d = \sqrt{(x_2 - x_1)^2 + (y_2 - y_1)^2} = $
$\sqrt{(3 - (-2))^2 + (-8 - 4)^2} = \sqrt{(5)^2 + (-12)^2} = \sqrt{25 + 144} = \sqrt{169} = 13$

29) $(x_1, y_1) = (6, -7)$ and $(x_2, y_2) = (-9, 1) \rightarrow d = \sqrt{(x_2 - x_1)^2 + (y_2 - y_1)^2} = $
$\sqrt{(-9 - 6)^2 + (1 - (-7))^2} = \sqrt{(-15)^2 + (8)^2} = \sqrt{225 + 64} = \sqrt{289} = 17$

30) $(x_1, y_1) = (8, -4)$ and $(x_2, y_2) = (-4, -20) \rightarrow d = \sqrt{(x_2 - x_1)^2 + (y_2 - y_1)^2} = $
$\sqrt{(-4 - 8)^2 + (-20 - (-4))^2} = \sqrt{(-12)^2 + (-16)^2} = \sqrt{144 + 256} = \sqrt{400} = 20$

31) $(x_1, y_1) = (5, 1)$ and $(x_2, y_2) = (9, -2) \rightarrow d = \sqrt{(x_2 - x_1)^2 + (y_2 - y_1)^2} = $
$\sqrt{(9 - 5)^2 + (-2 - 1)^2} = \sqrt{(4)^2 + (-3)^2} = \sqrt{16 + 9} = \sqrt{25} = 5$

32) $(x_1, y_1) = (-8, -17)$ and $(x_2, y_2) = (2, 7) \rightarrow d = \sqrt{(x_2 - x_1)^2 + (y_2 - y_1)^2} = $
$\sqrt{(2 - (-8))^2 + (7 - (-17))^2} = \sqrt{(10)^2 + (-24)^2} = \sqrt{100 + 576} = \sqrt{676} = 26$

33) $(x_1, y_1) = (18, 21)$ and $(x_2, y_2) = (-12, 5) \rightarrow d = \sqrt{(x_2 - x_1)^2 + (y_2 - y_1)^2} = $
$\sqrt{(-12 - 18)^2 + (5 - 21)^2} = \sqrt{(-30)^2 + (-16)^2} = \sqrt{900 + 256} = \sqrt{1,156} = 34$

DAY 8 **Polynomials**

Math topics that you'll learn in this chapter:

1. Simplifying Polynomials
2. Adding and Subtracting Polynomials
3. Multiplying Monomials
4. Multiplying and Dividing Monomials
5. Multiplying a Polynomial and a Monomial
6. Multiplying Binomials
7. Factoring Trinomials

Simplifying Polynomials

☆ To simplify Polynomials, find "like" terms. (they have same variables with same power).

☆ Use "FOIL". (First–Out–In–Last) for binomials:

$$(x + a)(x + b) = x^2 + (b + a)x + ab$$

☆ Add or Subtract "like" terms using order of operation.

Examples:

Example 1. Simplify this expression. $2x(3x - 4) - 6x =$

Solution: Use Distributive Property: $2x(3x - 4) = 6x^2 - 8x$

Now, combine like terms: $2x(3x - 4) - 6x = 6x^2 - 8x - 6x = 6x^2 - 14x$

Example 2. Simplify this expression. $(x + 5)(x + 7) =$

Solution: First, apply the FOIL method: $(a + b)(c + d) = ac + ad + bc + bd$

$(x + 5)(x + 7) = x^2 + 5x + 7x + 35$

Now combine like terms: $x^2 + 5x + 7x + 35 = x^2 + 12x + 35$

Example 3. Simplify this expression. $3x(-4x + 5) + 2x^2 - 5x =$

Solution: Use Distributive Property: $3x(-4x + 5) = -12x^2 + 15x$

Then: $3x(-4x + 5) + 2x^2 - 5x = -12x^2 + 15x + 2x^2 - 5x$

Now combine like terms: $-12x^2 + 2x^2 = -10x^2$, and $15x - 5x = 10x$

The simplified form of the expression: $-12x^2 + 15x + 2x^2 - 5x = -10x^2 + 10x$

Adding and Subtracting Polynomials

☆ Adding polynomials is just a matter of combining like terms, with some order of operations considerations thrown in.

☆ Be careful with the minus signs, and don't confuse addition and multiplication!

☆ For subtracting polynomials, sometimes you need to use the Distributive Property: $a(b + c) = ab + ac$, $a(b - c) = ab - ac$

Examples:

Example 1. Simplify the expressions. $(-5x^2 + 2x^3) - (-4x^3 + 2x^2) =$

Solution: First, use Distributive Property:
$-(-4x^3 + 2x^2) = 4x^3 - 2x^2$
$\rightarrow (-5x^2 + 2x^3) - (-4x^3 + 2x^2) = -5x^2 + 2x^3 + 4x^3 - 2x^2$
Now combine like terms: $2x^3 + 4x^3 = 6x^3$ and $-5x^2 - 2x^2 = -7x^2$
Then: $(x^2 - 2x^3) - (x^3 - 3x^2) = 6x^3 - 7x^2$

Example 2. Add expressions. $(2x^3 + 8) + (-x^3 + 4x^2) =$

Solution: Remove parentheses:
$$(2x^3 + 8) + (-x^3 + 4x^2) = 2x^3 + 8 - x^3 + 4x^2$$
Now combine like terms: $2x^3 + 8 - x^3 + 4x^2 = x^3 + 4x^2 + 8$

Example 3. Simplify the expressions. $(x^2 + 7x^3) - (11x^2 - 4x^3) =$

Solution: First, use Distributive Property: $-(11x^2 - 4x^3) = -11x^2 + 4x^3 \rightarrow$
$$(x^2 + 7x^3) - (11x^2 - 4x^3) = x^2 + 7x^3 - 11x^2 + 4x^3$$
Now combine like terms and write in standard form:
$x^2 + 7x^3 - 11x^2 + 4x^3 = 11x^3 - 10x^2$

Multiplying Monomials

☆ A monomial is a polynomial with just one term: Examples: $2x$ or $7y^2$.

☆ When you multiply monomials, first multiply the coefficients (a number placed before and multiplying the variable) and then multiply the variables using multiplication property of exponents.

$$x^a \times x^b = x^{a+b}$$

Examples:

Example 1. Multiply expressions. $3x^4y^5 \times 6x^2y^3$

Solution: Find the same variables and use multiplication property of exponents: $x^a \times x^b = x^{a+b}$
$x^4 \times x^2 = x^{4+2} = x^6$ and $y^5 \times y^3 = y^{5+3} = y^8$
Then, multiply coefficients and variables: $3x^4y^5 \times 6x^2y^3 = 18x^6y^8$

Example 2. Multiply expressions. $5a^5b^9 \times 3a^2b^8 =$

Solution: Use the multiplication property of exponents: $x^a \times x^b = x^{a+b}$
$a^5 \times a^2 = a^{5+2} = a^7$ and $b^9 \times b^8 = b^{9+8} = b^{17}$
Then: $5a^5b^9 \times 3a^2b^8 = 15a^7b^{17}$

Example 3. Multiply. $6x^3y^2z^4 \times 2x^2y^8z^6$

Solution: Use the multiplication property of exponents: $x^a \times x^b = x^{a+b}$
$x^3 \times x^2 = x^{3+2} = x^5$, $y^2 \times y^8 = y^{2+8} = y^{10}$ and $z^4 \times z^6 = z^{4+6} = z^{10}$
Then: $6x^3y^2z^4 \times 2x^2y^8z^6 = 12x^5y^{10}z^{10}$

Example 4. Simplify. $(2a^3b^6)(-5a^7b^{12}) =$

Solution: Use the multiplication property of exponents: $x^a \times x^b = x^{a+b}$
$a^3 \times a^7 = a^{3+7} = a^{10}$ and $b^6 \times b^{12} = b^{6+12} = b^{18}$
Then: $(2a^3b^6)(-5a^7b^{12}) = -10a^{10}b^{18}$

Multiplying and Dividing Monomials

☆ When you divide or multiply two monomials, you need to divide or multiply their coefficients and then divide or multiply their variables.

☆ In case of exponents with the same base, for Division, subtract their powers, for Multiplication, add their powers.

☆ Exponent's Multiplication and Division rules:

$$x^a \times x^b = x^{a+b} , \qquad \frac{x^a}{x^b} = x^{a-b}$$

Examples:

Example 1. Multiply expressions. $(5x^4)(3x^9) =$

Solution: Use multiplication property of exponents:
$x^a \times x^b = x^{a+b} \rightarrow x^4 \times x^9 = x^{13}$
Then: $(5x^4)(3x^9) = 15x^{13}$

Example 2. Divide expressions. $\frac{18x^3y^6}{9x^2y^4} =$

Solution: Use division property of exponents:
$\frac{x^a}{x^b} = x^{a-b} \rightarrow \frac{x^3}{x^2} = x^{3-2} = x^1$ and $\frac{y^6}{y^4} = y^{6-4} = y^2$
Then: $\frac{18x^3y^6}{9x^2y^4} = 2xy^2$

Example 3. Divide expressions. $\frac{51a^4b^{11}}{3a^2b^5}$

Solution: Use division property of exponents:
$\frac{x^a}{x^b} = x^{a-b} \rightarrow \frac{a^4}{a^2} = a^{4-2} = a^2$ and $\frac{b^{11}}{b^5} = b^{11-5} = b^6$
Then. $\frac{51a^4b^{11}}{3a^2b^5} = 17a^2b^6$

Multiplying a Polynomial and a Monomial

✰ When multiplying monomials, use the product rule for exponents.

$$x^a \times x^b = x^{a+b}$$

✰ When multiplying a monomial by a polynomial, use the distributive property.

$$a \times (b + c) = a \times b + a \times c = ab + ac$$
$$a \times (b - c) = a \times b - a \times c = ab - ac$$

Examples:

Example 1. Multiply expressions. $5x(4x + 7)$

Solution: Use Distributive Property:

$5x(4x + 7) = (5x \times 4x) + (5x \times 7) = 20x^2 + 35x$

Example 2. Multiply expressions. $y(2x^2 + 3y^2)$

Solution: Use Distributive Property:

$y(2x^2 + 3y^2) = y \times 2x^2 + y \times 3y^2 = 2x^2y + 3y^3$

Example 3. Multiply. $-2x(-x^2 + 3x + 6)$

Solution: Use Distributive Property:

$-2x(-x^2 + 3x + 6) = (-2x)(-x^2) + (-2x) \times (3x) + (-2x) \times (6) =$
Now simplify:

$(-2x)(-x^2) + (-2x) \times (3x) + (-2x) \times (6) = 2x^3 - 6x^2 - 12x$

Multiplying Binomials

☆ A binomial is a polynomial that is the sum or the difference of two terms, each of which is a monomial.

☆ To multiply two binomials, use the "FOIL" method. (First–Out–In–Last)

$$(x + a)(x + b) = x \times x + x \times b + a \times x + a \times b = x^2 + bx + ax + ab$$

Examples:

Example 1. Multiply Binomials. $(x - 5)(x + 4) =$

Solution: Use "FOIL". (First–Out–In–Last):

$(x - 5)(x + 4) = x^2 - 5x + 4x - 20$

Then combine like terms: $x^2 - 5x + 4x - 20 = x^2 - x - 20$

Example 2. Multiply. $(x + 3)(x + 6) =$

Solution: Use "FOIL". (First–Out–In–Last):

$(x + 3)(x + 6) = x^2 + 3x + 6x + 18$

Then simplify: $x^2 + 3x + 6x + 18 = x^2 + 9x + 18$

Example 3. Multiply. $(x - 8)(x + 4) =$

Solution: Use "FOIL". (First–Out–In–Last):

$(x - 8)(x + 4) = x^2 - 8x + 4x - 32$

Then simplify: $x^2 - 8x + 4x - 32 = x^2 - 4x - 32$

Example 4. Multiply Binomials. $(x - 6)(x - 3) =$

Solution: Use "FOIL". (First–Out–In–Last):

$(x - 6)(x - 3) = x^2 - 6x - 3x + 18$

Then combine like terms: $x^2 - 6x - 3x + 18 = x^2 - 9x + 18$

Factoring Trinomials

To factor trinomials, you can use following methods:

☆ "FOIL": $(x + a)(x + b) = x^2 + (b + a)x + ab$

☆ "Difference of Squares":

$$a^2 - b^2 = (a + b)(a - b)$$
$$a^2 + 2ab + b^2 = (a + b)(a + b)$$
$$a^2 - 2ab + b^2 = (a - b)(a - b)$$

☆ "Reverse FOIL": $x^2 + (b + a)x + ab = (x + a)(x + b)$

Examples:

Example 1. Factor this trinomial. $x^2 - 3x - 18$

Solution: Break the expression into groups. You need to find two numbers that their product is -18 and their sum is -3. (remember "Reverse FOIL": $x^2 + (b + a)x + ab = (x + a)(x + b)$). Those two numbers are 3 and -6. Then:
$$x^2 - 3x - 18 = (x^2 + 3x) + (-6x - 18)$$
Now factor out x from $x^2 + 3x : x(x + 3)$, and factor out -6 from
$-6x - 18: -6(x + 3)$; Then: $(x^2 + 3x) + (-6x - 18) = x(x + 3) - 6(x + 3)$
Now factor out like term: $(x + 3)$. Then: $(x + 3)(x - 6)$

Example 2. Factor this trinomial. $2x^2 - 4x - 48$

Solution: Break the expression into groups: $(2x^2 + 8x) + (-12x - 48)$
Now factor out $2x$ from $2x^2 + 8x : 2x(x + 4)$, and factor out -12 from
$-12x - 48: -12(x + 4)$; Then: $2x(x + 4) - 12(x + 4)$, now factor out like term:
$(x + 4) \rightarrow 2x(x + 4) - 12(x + 4) = (x + 4)(2x - 12)$

Day 8: Practices

✎ Simplify each polynomial.

1) $4(3x + 2) =$

2) $7(6x - 3) =$

3) $x(4x + 5) + 6x =$

4) $2x(x - 4) + 8x =$

5) $3(5x + 3) - 9x =$

6) $x(6x - 5) - 4x^2 + 11 =$

7) $-x^2 + 7 + 3x(x + 2) =$

8) $6x^2 - 7 + 3x(5x - 7) =$

✎ Add or subtract polynomials.

9) $(x^2 + 5) + (3x^2 - 2) =$

10) $(4x^2 - 5x) - (x^2 + 7x) =$

11) $(6x^3 - 2x^2) + (3x^3 - 7x^2) =$

12) $(6x^3 - 7x) - (9x^3 - 3x) =$

13) $(9x^3 + 5x^2) + (12x^2 - 7) =$

14) $(5x^3 - 8) - (2x^3 - 6x^2) =$

15) $(10x^3 + 4x) - (7x^3 - 5x) =$

16) $(12x^3 - 7x) - (3x^3 + 9x) =$

✎ Find the products. (Multiplying Monomials)

17) $5x^3 \times 6x^5 =$

18) $3x^4 \times 4x^3 =$

19) $-7a^3b \times 3a^2b^5 =$

20) $-5x^2y^3z \times 6x^6y^4z^5 =$

21) $-2a^3bc \times (-4a^8b^7) =$

22) $9u^6t^5 \times (-2u^2t) =$

23) $14x^2z \times 2x^6y^8z =$

24) $-12x^7y^6z \times 3xy^8 =$

25) $-9a^2b^3c \times 3a^7b^6 =$

26) $-11x^9y^7 \times (-6x^4y^3) =$

✎ **Simplify each expression. (Multiplying and Dividing Monomials)**

27) $(4x^3y^4)(2x^4y^3) =$

28) $(7x^2y^5)(3x^3y^6) =$

29) $(5x^9y^6)(8x^6y^9) =$

30) $(13a^4b^7)(2a^6b^9) =$

31) $\frac{54x^6y^3}{9x^4y} =$

32) $\frac{28x^5y^7}{4x^3y^4} =$

33) $\frac{32x^{17}y^{12}}{8x^{13}y^9} =$

34) $\frac{40x^7y^{19}}{5x^2y^{14}} =$

✎ **Find each product. (Multiplying a Polynomial and a Monomial)**

35) $6(4x - 2y) =$

36) $4x(5x + y) =$

37) $8x(x - 2y) =$

38) $x(3x^2 + 4x - 6) =$

39) $4x(2x^2 + 7x + 4) =$

40) $8x(3x^2 - 7x - 3) =$

✎ **Find each product. (Multiplying Binomials)**

41) $(x - 4)(x + 5) =$

42) $(x - 3)(x + 3) =$

43) $(x + 8)(x + 7) =$

44) $(x - 5)(x + 9) =$

45) $(2x + 4)(x - 6) =$

46) $(2x - 11)(x + 6) =$

✎ **Factor each trinomial.**

47) $x^2 + 2x - 15 =$

48) $x^2 - x - 42 =$

49) $x^2 - 14x + 49 =$

50) $x^2 - 7x - 60 =$

51) $2x^2 + 6x - 20 =$

52) $3x^2 + 13x - 10 =$

Day 8: Answers

1) $4(3x + 2) = (4 \times 3x) + (4 \times 2) = 12x + 8$

2) $7(6x - 3) = (7 \times 6x) - (7 \times 3) = 42x - 21$

3) $x(4x + 5) + 6x = (x \times 4x) + (x \times 5) + 6x = 4x^2 + 5x + 6x = 4x^2 + 11x$

4) $2x(x - 4) + 8x = (2x \times x) + \left(2x \times (-4)\right) + 8x = 2x^2 - 8x + 8x = 2x^2$

5) $3(5x + 3) - 9x = (3 \times 5x) + (3 \times 3) - 9x = 15x - 9x + 9 = 6x + 9$

6) $x(6x - 5) - 4x^2 + 11 = (x \times 6x) + \left(x \times (-5)\right) - 4x^2 + 11 =$

   $6x^2 - 4x^2 - 5x + 11 = 2x^2 - 5x + 11$

7) $-x^2 + 7 + 3x(x + 2) = -x^2 + 7 + (3x \times x) + (3x \times 2) = -x^2 + 7 + 3x^2 + 6x =$

   $2x^2 + 6x + 7$

8) $6x^2 - 7 + 3x(5x - 7) = 6x^2 - 7 + (3x \times 5x) + \left(3x \times (-7)\right) =$

   $6x^2 - 7 + 15x^2 - 21x = 21x^2 - 21x - 7$

9) $(x^2 + 5) + (3x^2 - 2) = x^2 + 3x^2 + 5 - 2 = 4x^2 + 3$

10) $(4x^2 - 5x) - (x^2 + 7x) = 4x^2 - x^2 - 5x - 7x = 3x^2 - 12x$

11) $(6x^3 - 2x^2) + (3x^3 - 7x^2) = 6x^3 + 3x^3 - 2x^2 - 7x^2 = 9x^3 - 9x^2$

12) $(6x^3 - 7x) - (9x^3 - 3x) = 6x^3 - 9x^3 - 7x + 3x = -3x^3 - 4x$

13) $(9x^3 + 5x^2) + (12x^2 - 7) = 9x^3 + 5x^2 + 12x^2 - 7 = 9x^3 + 17x^2 - 7$

14) $(5x^3 - 8) - (2x^3 - 6x^2) = 5x^3 - 2x^3 + 6x^2 - 8 = 3x^3 + 6x^2 - 8$

15) $(10x^3 + 4x) - (7x^3 - 5x) = 10x^3 - 7x^3 + 4x + 5x = 3x^3 + 9x$

16) $(12x^3 - 7x) - (3x^3 + 9x) = 12x^3 - 3x^3 - 7x - 9x = 9x^3 - 16x$

17) $5x^3 \times 6x^5 \rightarrow 5 \times 6 = 30, \; x^3 \times x^5 = x^{3+5} = x^8 \rightarrow 5x^3 \times 6x^5 = 30x^8$

18) $3x^4 \times 4x^3 \rightarrow 3 \times 4 = 12, \; x^4 \times x^3 = x^{4+3} = x^7 \rightarrow 3x^4 \times 4x^3 = 12x^7$

19) $-7a^3b \times 3a^2b^5 \rightarrow -7 \times 3 = -21, \; a^3 \times a^2 = a^{3+2} = a^5, \; b \times b^5 = b^{1+5} = b^6 \rightarrow$

   $-7a^3b \times 3a^2b^5 = -21a^5b^6$

20) $-5x^2y^3z \times 6x^6y^4z^5 \rightarrow -5 \times 6 = -30, \; x^2 \times x^6 = x^{2+6} = x^8, y^3 \times y^4 = y^{3+4} = y^7,$

   $z \times z^5 = z^{1+5} = z^6 \rightarrow -5x^2y^3z \times 6x^6y^4z^5 = -30x^8y^7z^6$

21) $-2a^3bc \times (-4a^8b^7) \rightarrow -2 \times (-4) = 8$, $a^3 \times a^8 = a^{3+8} = a^{11}$, $b \times b^7 = b^{1+7} = b^8 \rightarrow -2a^3bc \times (-4a^8b^7) = 8a^{11}b^8c$

22) $9u^6t^5 \times (-2u^2t) \rightarrow 9 \times (-2) = -18$, $u^6 \times u^2 = u^{6+2} = u^8$, $t^5 \times t^1 = t^{5+1} = t^6 \rightarrow 9u^6t^5 \times (-2u^2t) = -18u^8t^6$

23) $14x^2z \times 2x^6y^8z \rightarrow 14 \times 2 = 28$, $x^2 \times x^6 = x^{2+6} = x^8$, $z \times z = z^{1+1} = z^2 \rightarrow 14x^2z \times 2x^6y^8z = 28x^8y^8z^2$

24) $-12x^7y^6z \times 3xy^8 \rightarrow -12 \times 3 = -36$, $x^7 \times x = x^{1+7} = x^8$, $y^6 \times y^8 = y^{6+8} = y^{14} \rightarrow -12x^7y^6z \times 3xy^8 = -36x^8y^{14}z$

25) $-9a^2b^3c \times 3a^7b^6 \rightarrow -9 \times 3 = -27$, $a^2 \times a^7 = a^{2+7} = a^9$, $b^3 \times b^6 = b^{3+6} = b^9 \rightarrow -9a^2b^3c \times 3a^7b^6 = -27a^9b^9c$

26) $-11x^9y^7 \times (-6x^4y^3) \rightarrow -11 \times (-6) = 66$, $x^9 \times x^4 = x^{9+4} = x^{13}$, $y^7 \times y^3 = y^{7+3} = y^{10} \rightarrow -11x^9y^7 \times (-6x^4y^3) = 66x^{13}y^{10}$

27) $(4x^3y^4)(2x^4y^3) \rightarrow 4 \times 2 = 8$, $x^3 \times x^4 = x^{3+4} = x^7$, $y^4 \times y^3 = y^{4+3} = y^7 \rightarrow (4x^3y^4)(2x^4y^3) = 8x^7y^7$

28) $(7x^2y^5)(3x^3y^6) \rightarrow 7 \times 3 = 21$, $x^2 \times x^3 = x^{2+3} = x^5$, $y^5 \times y^6 = y^{5+6} = y^{11} \rightarrow (7x^2y^5)(3x^3y^6) = 21x^5y^{11}$

29) $(5x^9y^6)(8x^6y^9) \rightarrow 5 \times 8 = 40$, $x^9 \times x^6 = x^{9+6} = x^{15}$, $y^6 \times y^9 = y^{6+9} = y^{15} \rightarrow (5x^9y^6)(8x^6y^9) = 40x^{15}y^{15}$

30) $(13a^4b^7)(2a^6b^9) \rightarrow 13 \times 2 = 26$, $a^4 \times a^6 = a^{4+6} = a^{10}$, $b^7 \times b^9 = b^{7+9} = b^{16} \rightarrow (13a^4b^7)(2a^6b^9) = 26a^{10}b^{16}$

31) $\frac{54x^6y^3}{9x^4y} \rightarrow \frac{54}{9} = 6$, $\frac{x^6}{x^4} = x^{6-4} = x^2$, $\frac{y^3}{y} = y^{3-1} = y^2 \rightarrow \frac{54x^6y^3}{9x^4y} = 6x^2y^2$

32) $\frac{28x^5y^7}{4x^3y^4} \rightarrow \frac{28}{4} = 7$, $\frac{x^5}{x^3} = x^{5-3} = x^2$, $\frac{y^7}{y^4} = y^{7-4} = y^3 \rightarrow \frac{28x^5y^7}{4x^3y^4} = 7x^2y^3$

33) $\frac{32x^{17}y^{12}}{8x^{13}y^9} \rightarrow \frac{32}{8} = 4$, $\frac{x^{17}}{x^{13}} = x^{17-13} = x^4$, $\frac{y^{12}}{y^9} = y^{12-9} = y^3 \rightarrow \frac{32x^{17}y^{12}}{8x^{13}y^9} = 4x^4y^3$

34) $\frac{40x^7y^{19}}{5x^2y^{14}} = \rightarrow \frac{40}{5} = 8$, $\frac{x^7}{x^2} = x^{7-2} = x^5$, $\frac{y^{19}}{y^{14}} = y^{19-14} = y^5 \rightarrow \frac{40x^7y^{19}}{5x^2y^{14}} = 8x^5y^5$

35) $6(4x - 2y) = (6 \times 4x) - (6 \times 2y) = 24x - 12y$

36) $4x(5x + y) = (4x \times 5x) + (4x \times y) = 20x^2 + 4xy$

37) $8x(x - 2y) = (8x \times x) - (8x \times 2y) = 8x^2 - 16xy$

38) $x(3x^2 + 4x - 6) = (x \times 3x^2) + (x \times 4x) + (x \times (-6)) = 3x^3 + 4x^2 - 6x$

39) $4x(2x^2 + 7x + 4) = (4x \times 2x^2) + (4x \times 7x) + (4x \times 4) = 8x^3 + 28x^2 + 16x$

40) $8x(3x^2 - 7x - 3) = (8x \times 3x^2) + (8x \times (-7x)) + (8x \times (-3)) = 24x^3 - 56x^2 - 24x$

41) $(x - 4)(x + 5) = (x \times x) + (x \times 5) + (-4 \times x) + (-4 \times 5) = x^2 + 5x - 4x - 20 =$
$x^2 + x - 20$

42) $(x - 3)(x + 3) = (x \times x) + (x \times 3) + (-3 \times x) + (-3 \times 3) = x^2 + 3x - 3x - 9 = x^2 - 9$

43) $(x + 8)(x + 7) = (x \times x) + (x \times 7) + (8 \times x) + (8 \times 7) = x^2 + 7x + 8x + 56 =$
$x^2 + 15x + 56$

44) $(x - 5)(x + 9) = (x \times x) + (x \times 9) + (-5 \times x) + (-5 \times 9) = x^2 + 9x - 5x - 45 =$
$x^2 + 4x - 45$

45) $(2x + 4)(x - 6) = (2x \times x) + (2x \times (-6)) + (4 \times x) + (4 \times (-6)) =$
$2x^2 - 12x + 4x - 24 = 2x^2 - 8x - 24$

46) $(2x - 11)(x + 6) = (2x \times x) + (2x \times 6) + ((-11) \times x) + ((-11) \times 6) =$
$2x^2 + 12x - 11x - 66 = 2x^2 + x - 66$

47) $x^2 + 2x - 15 \rightarrow$(Use this rule: $x^2 + (b + a)x + ab = (x + a)(x + b)$). Then:
$x^2 + 2x - 15 = x^2 + (5 - 3)x + (5 \times (-3)) = (x + 5)(x - 3)$

48) $x^2 - x - 42 = x^2 + (-7 + 6)x + ((-7) \times 6) = (x - 7)(x + 6)$

49) $x^2 - 14x + 49 = x^2 + (-7 - 7)x + ((-7) \times (-7)) = (x - 7)(x - 7)$

50) $x^2 - 7x - 60x^2 = x^2 + (-12 + 5)x + ((-12) \times 5) = (x - 12)(x + 5)$

51) $2x^2 + 6x - 20 = 2x^2 + (10x - 4x) - 20 = (2x^2 + 10x) + (-4x - 20) =$
$2x(x + 5) - 4(x + 5) = (2x - 4)(x + 5)$

52) $3x^2 + 13x - 10 = (3x^2 + 15x) + (-2x - 10) = 3x(x + 5) - 2(x + 5) =$
$(3x - 2)(x + 5)$

DAY 9 Geometry and Solid Figures

Math topics that you'll learn in this chapter:

1. The Pythagorean Theorem
2. Complementary and Supplementary angles
3. Parallel lines and Transversals
4. Triangles
5. Special Right Triangles
6. Polygons
7. Circles
8. Trapezoids
9. Cubes
10. Rectangle Prisms
11. Cylinder

107

The Pythagorean Theorem

☆ You can use the Pythagorean Theorem to find a missing side in a right triangle.

☆ In any right triangle: $a^2 + b^2 = c^2$

Examples:

Example 1. Right triangle ABC (not shown) has two legs of lengths 3 cm (AB) and 4 cm (AC). What is the length of the hypotenuse of the triangle (side BC)?

Solution: Use Pythagorean Theorem: $a^2 + b^2 = c^2$, $a = 3$ and $b = 4$

Then: $a^2 + b^2 = c^2 \rightarrow 3^2 + 4^2 = c^2 \rightarrow 9 + 16 = c^2 \rightarrow 25 = c^2 \rightarrow c = \sqrt{25} = 5$

The length of the hypotenuse is 5 cm.

Example 2. Find the hypotenuse of this triangle.

Solution: Use Pythagorean Theorem: $a^2 + b^2 = c^2$

Then: $a^2 + b^2 = c^2 \rightarrow 15^2 + 8^2 = c^2 \rightarrow 225 + 64 = c^2$

$c^2 = 289 \rightarrow c = \sqrt{289} = 17$

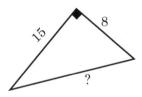

Example 3. Find the length of the missing side in this triangle.

Solution: Use Pythagorean Theorem: $a^2 + b^2 = c^2$

Then: $a^2 + b^2 = c^2 \rightarrow 20^2 + b^2 = 25^2 \rightarrow 400 + b^2 = 625 \rightarrow$

$b^2 = 625 - 400 \rightarrow b^2 = 225 \rightarrow b = \sqrt{225} = 15$

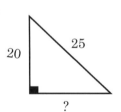

Complementary and Supplementary angles

☆ Two angles with a sum of 90 degrees are called complementary angles.

☆ Two angles with a sum of 180 degrees are Supplementary angles.

Examples:

Example 1. Find the missing angle.

Solution: Notice that the two angles form a right angle. This means that the angles are complementary, and their sum is 90. Then: $22° + x = 90° \rightarrow x = 90° - 22° = 68°$
The missing angle is 68 degrees. $x = 68°$

Example 2. Angles Q and S are supplementary. What is the measure of angle Q if angle S is 45 degrees?

Solution: Q and S are supplementary $\rightarrow Q + S = 180 \rightarrow Q + 45 = 180 \rightarrow$
$$Q = 180 - 45 = 135°$$

Example 3. Angles x and y are complementary. What is the measure of angle x if angle y is 27 degrees?

Solution: Angles x and y are complementary $\rightarrow x + y = 90 \rightarrow x + 27 = 90 \rightarrow$
$$x = 90 - 27 = 63°$$

Parallel lines and Transversals

✩ When a line (transversal) intersects two parallel lines in the same plane, eight angles are formed. In the following diagram, a transversal intersects two parallel lines. Angles 1, 3, 5 and 7 are congruent. Angles 2, 4, 6, and 8 are also congruent.

✩ In the following diagram, the following angles are supplementary angles (their sum is 180):

❖ Angles 1 and 8

❖ Angles 2 and 7

❖ Angles 3 and 6

❖ Angles 4 and 5

Example:

In the following diagram, two parallel lines are cut by a transversal. What is the value of x?

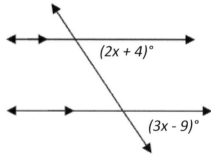

Solution: The two angles $2x + 4$ and $3x - 9$ are equivalent.

That is: $2x + 4 = 3x - 9$

Now, solve for x:

$2x + 4 + 9 = 3x - 9 + 9$

$\rightarrow 2x + 13 = 3x \rightarrow 2x + 13 - 2x = 3x - 2x \rightarrow$

$13 = x$

Triangles

★ In any triangle, the sum of all angles is 180 degrees.

★ Area of a triangle $= \frac{1}{2}$(base×height)

Examples:

Example 1. What is the area of this triangles?

Solution: Use the area formula:

Area$= \frac{1}{2}$(base×height)

base$=$ 18 and height$=$ 9, Then:

Area$= \frac{1}{2}(18 \times 9) = \frac{162}{2} = 81$

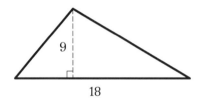

Example 2. What is the area of this triangles?

Solution: Use the area formula:

Area$= \frac{1}{2}$(base×height)

base$=$ 18 and height$=$ 7; Area$= \frac{1}{2}(18 \times 7) = \frac{126}{2} = 63$

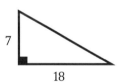

Example 3. What is the missing angle in this triangle?

Solution: In any triangle, the sum of all angles is 180 degrees. Let x be the missing angle.

Then: $63 + 84 + x = 180 \rightarrow 147 + x = 180 \rightarrow$

$\qquad x = 180 - 147 = 33^{\circ}$

The missing angle is 33 degrees.

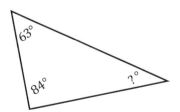

Special Right Triangles

✩ A special right triangle is a triangle whose sides are in a particular ratio. Two special right triangles are $45° - 45° - 90°$ and $30° - 60° - 90°$ triangles.

✩ In a special $45° - 45° - 90°$ triangle, the three angles are $45°$, $45°$ and $90°$. The lengths of the sides of this triangle are in the ratio of $1:1:\sqrt{2}$.

✩ In a special triangle $30° - 60° - 90°$, the three angles are $30° - 60° - 90°$. The lengths of this triangle are in the ratio of $1:\sqrt{3}:2$.

Examples:

Example 1. Find the length of the hypotenuse of a right triangle if the length of the other two sides are both 6 inches.

Solution: This is a right triangle with two equal sides. Therefore, it must be a $45° - 45° - 90°$ triangle. Two equivalent sides are 6 inches. The ratio of sides: $x:x:x\sqrt{2}$
The length of the hypotenuse is $6\sqrt{2}$ inches. $x:x:x\sqrt{2} \rightarrow 6:6:6\sqrt{2}$

Example 2. The length of the hypotenuse of a right triangle is 6 inches. What are the lengths of the other two sides if one angle of the triangle is $30°$?

Solution: The hypotenuse is 6 inches and the triangle is a $30° - 60° - 90°$ triangle. Then, one side of the triangle is 3 (it's half the side of the hypotenuse) and the other side is $3\sqrt{3}$. (it's the smallest side times $\sqrt{3}$)
$x:x\sqrt{3}:2x \rightarrow x = 3 \rightarrow x:x\sqrt{3}:2x = 3:3\sqrt{3}:6$

Polygons

★ The perimeter of a square = $4 \times side = 4s$

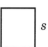

★ The perimeter of a rectangle = $2(width + length)$

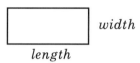

★ The perimeter of trapezoid = $a + b + c + d$

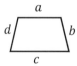

★ The perimeter of a regular hexagon = $6a$

★ The perimeter of a parallelogram = $2(l + w)$

Examples:

Example 1. Find the perimeter of following regular hexagon.

Solution: Since the hexagon is regular, all sides are equal.
Then, the perimeter of the hexagon = $6 \times (one\ side)$
The perimeter of the hexagon = $6 \times (one\ side) = 6 \times 7 = 42\ m$

Example 2. Find the perimeter of following trapezoid.

Solution: The perimeter of a trapezoid = $a + b + c + d$
The perimeter of the trapezoid = $9 + 7 + 13 + 7 = 36\ ft$

Circles

✫ In a circle, variable r is usually used for the radius and d for diameter.

✫ *Area of a circle* $= \pi r^2$ (π is about 3.14)

✫ *Circumference of a circle* $= 2\pi r$

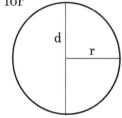

Examples:

Example 1. Find the area of this circle. ($\pi = 3.14$)

Solution:
Use area formula: $Area = \pi r^2$
$r = 5\ in \rightarrow Area = \pi(5)^2 = 25\pi$, $\pi = 3.14$
Then: $Area = 25 \times 3.14 = 78.5\ in^2$

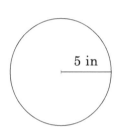

Example 2. Find the Circumference of this circle. ($\pi = 3.14$)

Solution:
Use Circumference formula: $Circumference = 2\pi r$
$r = 7\ cm \rightarrow Circumference = 2\pi(7) = 14\pi$
$\pi = 3.14$, Then: $Circumference = 14 \times 3.14 = 43.96\ cm$

Example 3. Find the area of this circle.

Solution:
Use area formula: $Area = \pi r^2$
$r = 11\ in$, Then: $Area = \pi(11)^2 = 121\pi$, $\pi = 3.14$
$Area = 121 \times 3.14 = 379.94\ in^2$

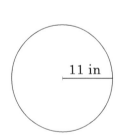

Trapezoids

✯ A quadrilateral with at least one pair of parallel sides is a trapezoid.

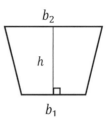

✯ Area of a trapezoid $= \frac{1}{2}h(b_1 + b_2)$

Examples:

Example 1. Calculate the area of this trapezoid.

Solution:

Use area formula: $A = \frac{1}{2}h(b_1 + b_2)$

$b_1 = 5\ cm$, $b_2 = 9\ cm$ and $h = 16\ cm$

Then: $A = \frac{1}{2}(16)(9 + 5) = 8(14) = 112\ cm^2$

Example 2. Calculate the area of this trapezoid.

Solution:

Use area formula: $A = \frac{1}{2}h(b_1 + b_2)$

$b_1 = 8\ cm$, $b_2 = 16\ cm$ and $h = 12\ cm$

Then: $A = \frac{1}{2}(12)(8 + 16) = 144\ cm^2$

Cubes

☆ A cube is a three-dimensional solid object bounded by six square sides.

☆ Volume is the measure of the amount of space inside of a solid figure, like a cube, ball, cylinder or pyramid.

☆ The volume of a cube = $(one\ side)^3$

☆ The surface area of a cube = $6 \times (one\ side)^2$

Examples:

Example 1. Find the volume and surface area of this cube.

Solution: Use volume formula: $volume = (one\ side)^3$
Then: $volume = (one\ side)^3 = (5)^3 = 125\ cm^3$
Use surface area formula:
$surface\ area\ of\ a\ cube: 6(one\ side)^2 = 6(5)^2 = 6(25) = 150\ cm^2$

5 cm

Example 2. Find the volume and surface area of this cube.

Solution: Use volume formula: $volume = (one\ side)^3$
Then: $volume = (one\ side)^3 = (7)^3 = 343\ cm^3$
Use surface area formula:
$surface\ area\ of\ a\ cube: 6(one\ side)^2 = 6(7)^2 = 6(49) = 294\ cm^2$

7 cm

Example 3. Find the volume and surface area of this cube.

Solution: Use volume formula: $volume = (one\ side)^3$
Then: $volume = (one\ side)^3 = (9)^3 = 729\ m^3$
Use surface area formula:
$surface\ area\ of\ a\ cube: 6(one\ side)^2 = 6(9)^2 = 6(81) = 486\ m^2$

9 m

Rectangular Prisms

✩ A rectangular prism is a solid 3-dimensional object with six rectangular faces.

✩ The volume of a Rectangular prism = *Length × Width × Height*

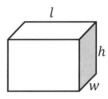

$Volume = l \times w \times h$

$Surface\ area = 2 \times (wh + lw + lh)$

Examples:

Example 1. Find the volume and surface area of this rectangular prism.

Solution: Use volume formula: $Volume = l \times w \times h$

Then: $Volume = 9 \times 7 \times 10 = 630\ m^3$

Use surface area formula: $Surface\ area = 2 \times (wh + lw + lh)$

Then: $Surface\ area = 2 \times \big((7 \times 10) + (9 \times 7) + (9 \times 10)\big)$

$\qquad = 2 \times (70 + 63 + 90) = 2 \times (223) = 446\ m^2$

Example 2. Find the volume and surface area of this rectangular prism.

Solution: Use volume formula: $Volume = l \times w \times h$

Then: $Volume = 8 \times 5 \times 11 = 440\ m^3$

Use surface area formula: $Surface\ area = 2 \times (wh + lw + lh)$

Then: $Surface\ area = 2 \times \big((5 \times 11) + (8 \times 5) + (8 \times 11)\big)$

$\qquad = 2 \times (55 + 40 + 88) = 2 \times (183) = 366\ m^2$

Cylinder

☆ A cylinder is a solid geometric figure with straight parallel sides and a circular or oval cross-section.

☆ *Volume of a Cylinder* $= \pi(radius)^2 \times height$, $\pi \approx 3.14$

☆ *Surface area of a cylinder* $= 2\pi r^2 + 2\pi rh$

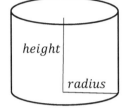

Examples:

Example 1. Find the volume and Surface area of the follow Cylinder.

Solution: Use volume formula:

$Volume = \pi(radius)^2 \times height$

Then: $Volume = \pi(6)^2 \times 12 = 36\pi \times 12 = 432\pi$

$\pi = 3.14$, then: $Volume = 432\pi = 432 \times 3.14 = 1,356.48 \ cm^3$

Use surface area formula: $Surface \ area = 2\pi r^2 + 2\pi rh$

Then: $2\pi(6)^2 + 2\pi(6)(12) = 2\pi(36) + 2\pi(72) = 72\pi + 144\pi = 216\pi$

$\pi = 3.14$, Then: $Surface \ area = 216 \times 3.14 = 678.24 \ cm^2$

Example 2. Find the volume and Surface area of the follow Cylinder.

Solution: Use volume formula:

$Volume = \pi(radius)^2 \times height$

Then: $Volume = \pi(2)^2 \times 5 = 4\pi \times 5 = 20\pi$

$\pi = 3.14$, Then: $Volume = 20\pi = 62.8 \ cm^3$

Use surface area formula: $Surface \ area = 2\pi r^2 + 2\pi rh$

Then: $= 2\pi(2)^2 + 2\pi(2)(5) = 2\pi(4) + 2\pi(10) = 8\pi + 20\pi = 28\pi$

$\pi = 3.14$, then: $Surface \ area = 28 \times 3.14 = 87.92 \ cm^2$

Day 9: Practices

✍ Find the missing side?

1)

2)

3)

4)
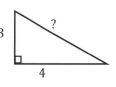

✍ Find the measure of the unknown angle in each triangle.

5)

6)

7)
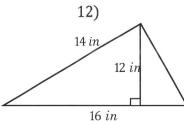

8)

✍ Find the area of each triangle.

9)

10)

11)

12)
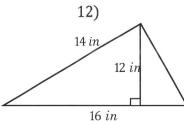

✍ Find the perimeter or circumference of each shape.

13)

14)

15)

16) regular hexagon
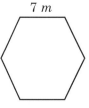

✎ **Find the area of each trapezoid.**

17)   18)   19)   20)

✎ **Find the volume of each cube.**

21)   22)   23)   24)

✎ **Find the volume of each Rectangular Prism.**

25)   26)   27)

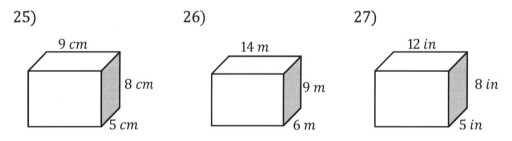

✎ **Find the volume of each Cylinder. Round your answer to the nearest tenth. ($\pi = 3.14$)**

28)   29)   30)

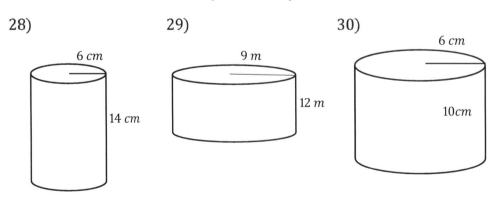

Day 9: Answers

1) Use Pythagorean Theorem: $a^2 + b^2 = c^2$, $a = 6$ and $c = 10$, Then: $6^2 + b^2 = 10^2 \rightarrow 36 + b^2 = 100 \rightarrow b^2 = 100 - 36 = 64 \rightarrow b = \sqrt{64} = 8$

2) Use Pythagorean Theorem: $a^2 + b^2 = c^2$, $a = 15$ and $b = 8$, Then: $15^2 + 8^2 = c^2 \rightarrow 225 + 64 = c^2 \rightarrow c^2 = 289 \rightarrow c = \sqrt{289} = 17$

3) Use Pythagorean Theorem: $a^2 + b^2 = c^2$, $a = 12$ and $c = 13$, Then: $12^2 + b^2 = 13^2 \rightarrow 144 + b^2 = 169 \rightarrow b^2 = 169 - 144 = 25 \rightarrow b = \sqrt{25} = 5$

4) Use Pythagorean Theorem: $a^2 + b^2 = c^2$, $a = 3$ and $b = 4$, Then: $3^2 + 4^2 = c^2 \rightarrow 9 + 16 = c^2 \rightarrow c^2 = 25 \rightarrow c = \sqrt{25} = 5$

5) In any triangle, the sum of all angles is 180 degrees. Then: $85 + 40 + x = 180 \rightarrow 125 + x = 180 \rightarrow x = 180 - 125 = 55$

6) $58 + 42 + x = 180 \rightarrow 100 + x = 180 \rightarrow x = 180 - 100 = 80$

7) $71 + 18 + x = 180 \rightarrow 89 + x = 180 \rightarrow x = 180 - 89 = 91$

8) $28 + 68 + x = 180 \rightarrow 96 + x = 180 \rightarrow x = 180 - 96 = 84$

9) Area $= \frac{1}{2}$(base×height), base= 8 and height = 5; Area $= \frac{1}{2}(8 \times 5) = \frac{40}{2} = 20 \, ft^2$

10) Base = 7 m and height = 12 m; Area $= \frac{1}{2}(12 \times 7) = \frac{84}{2} = 42 \, m^2$

11) Base = 12 cm and height = 6 cm; Area $= \frac{1}{2}(12 \times 6) = \frac{72}{2} = 36 \, cm^2$

12) Base = 16 in and height = 12 in; Area $= \frac{1}{2}(16 \times 12) = \frac{192}{2} = 96 \, in^2$

13) The perimeter of a parallelogram $= 2(l + w) \rightarrow l = 14 \, cm, w = 16 \, cm$.
   Then: $2(l + w) = 2(14 + 16) = 60 \, cm$

14) The perimeter of a rectangle $= 2(w + l) \rightarrow l = 10 \, ft, w = 8 \, ft$.
   Then: $2(l + w) = 2(10 + 8) = 36 \, ft$

15) Circumference of a circle $= 2\pi r \rightarrow r = 9 \, in$. Then: $2\pi \times 9 = 18 \times 3.14 = 56.52 \, in$

16) The perimeter of a regular hexagon $= 6a \rightarrow a = 7 \, m$. Then: $6 \times 7 = 42 \, m$

17) The area of a trapezoid $= \frac{1}{2}h(b_1 + b_2) \rightarrow b_1 = 12\ m$, $b_2 = 15\ m$ and $h = 8m$.

Then: $A = \frac{1}{2}(8)(12 + 15) = 108\ m^2$

18) $b_1 = 10\ cm$, $b_2 = 14\ cm$ and $h = 6\ cm$. Then: $A = \frac{1}{2}(6)(10 + 14) = 72\ cm^2$

19) $b_1 = 9\ ft$, $b_2 = 13\ ft$ and $h = 7\ ft$. Then: $A = \frac{1}{2}(7)(9 + 13) = 77\ ft^2$

20) $b_1 = 8\ cm$, $b_2 = 12\ cm$ and $h = 6\ cm$. Then: $A = \frac{1}{2}(6)(8 + 12) = 60\ cm^2$

21) The volume of a cube $= (one\ side)^3 = (5)^3 = 125\ cm^3$

22) The volume of a cube $= (one\ side)^3 = (30)^3 = 27,000\ ft^3$

23) The volume of a cube $= (one\ side)^3 = (11)^3 = 1,331\ in^3$

24) The volume of a cube $= (one\ side)^3 = (7)^3 = 343\ miles^3$

25) The volume of a Rectangular prism $= l \times w \times h \rightarrow l = 9\ cm$, $w = 5\ cm$, $h = 8\ cm$.

Then: $V = 9 \times 5 \times 8 = 360\ cm^3$

26) $V = l \times w \times h \rightarrow l = 14\ m$, $w = 6\ m$, $h = 9\ m$. Then: $V = 14 \times 6 \times 9 = 756\ m^3$

27) $V = l \times w \times h \rightarrow l = 12\ in$, $w = 5\ in$, $h = 8\ in$. Then: $V = 12 \times 5 \times 8 = 480\ in^3$

28) Volume of a Cylinder $= \pi(r)^2 \times h \rightarrow r = 6\ cm$, $h = 14\ cm$

Then: $\pi(6)^2 \times 14 = 3.14 \times 36 \times 14 = 1,582.56 \approx 1,582.6$

29) Volume of a Cylinder $= \pi(r)^2 \times h \rightarrow r = 9\ m$, $h = 12\ m$

Then: $\pi(9)^2 \times 12 = 3.14 \times 81 \times 12 = 3,052.08 \approx 3,052.1$

30) Volume of a Cylinder $= \pi(r)^2 \times h \rightarrow r = 6\ cm$, $h = 10\ cm$

Then: $\pi(6)^2 \times 10 = 3.14 \times 36 \times 10 = 1,130$

DAY 10 Statistics and Functions

Math topics that you'll learn in this chapter:

1. Mean, Median, Mode, and Range of the Given Data
2. Pie Graph
3. Probability Problems
4. Permutations and Combinations
5. Function Notation and Evaluation
6. Adding and Subtracting Functions
7. Multiplying and Dividing Functions
8. Compositions of Functions

125

Mean, Median, Mode, and Range of the Given Data

☆ **Mean:** $\dfrac{sum\ of\ the\ data}{total\ number\ of\ data\ entires}$

☆ **Mode:** the value in the list that appears most often

☆ **Median:** is the middle number of a group of numbers arranged in order by size.

☆ **Range:** the difference of the largest value and smallest value in the list

Examples:

Example 1. What is the mode of these numbers? 4, 7, 8, 7, 8, 9, 8, 5

Solution: Mode: the value in the list that appears most often.
Therefore, the mode is number 8. There are three number 8 in the data.

Example 2. What is the median of these numbers? $6, 11, 15, 10, 17, 20, 7$

Solution: Write the numbers in order: $6, 7, 10, 11, 15, 17, 20$
The median is the number in the middle. Therefore, the median is 11.

Example 3. What is the mean of these numbers? $8, 5, 3, 7, 6, 4, 9$

Solution: Mean: $\dfrac{sum\ of\ the\ data}{total\ number\ of\ data\ entires} = \dfrac{8+5+3+7+6+4+9}{7} = \dfrac{42}{7} = 6$

Example 4. What is the range in this list? $9, 2, 5, 10, 15, 22, 7$

Solution: Range is the difference of the largest value and smallest value in the list. The largest value is 22 and the smallest value is 2.
Then: $22 - 2 = 20$

Pie Graph

☆ A Pie Graph (Pie Chart) is a circle chart divided into sectors, each sector represents the relative size of each value.

☆ Pie charts represent a snapshot of how a group is broken down into smaller pieces.

Example:

A library has 650 books that include Mathematics, Physics, Chemistry, English and History. Use the following graph to answer the questions.

Example 1. What is the number of Mathematics books?

Solution: Number of total books = 650

Percent of Mathematics books = 32%

Then, the number of Mathematics books: $32\% \times 650 = 0.32 \times 650 = 208$

Example 2. What is the number of History books?

Solution: Number of total books = 650

Percent of History books = 10%

Then: $0.10 \times 650 = 65$

Example 3. What is the number of English books in the library?

Solution: Number of total books = 650

Percent of English books = 14%

Then: $0.14 \times 650 = 91$

Probability Problems

☆ Probability is the likelihood of something happening in the future. It is expressed as a number between zero (can never happen) to 1 (will always happen).

☆ Probability can be expressed as a fraction, a decimal, or a percent.

☆ Probability formula: $Probability = \frac{number\ of\ desired\ outcomes}{number\ of\ total\ outcomes}$

Examples:

Example 1. Anita's trick–or–treat bag contains 8 pieces of chocolate, 16 suckers, 22 pieces of gum and 20 pieces of licorice. If she randomly pulls a piece of candy from her bag, what is the probability of her pulling out a piece of gum?

Solution: Probability $= \frac{number\ of\ desired\ outcomes}{number\ of\ total\ outcomes}$

Probability of pulling out a piece of gum $= \frac{22}{8+16+22+20} = \frac{22}{66} = \frac{1}{3}$

Example 2. A bag contains 25 balls: five green, eight black, seven blue, a brown, a red and three white. If 24 balls are removed from the bag at random, what is the probability that a red ball has been removed?

Solution: If 24 balls are removed from the bag at random, there will be one ball in the bag. The probability of choosing a red ball is 1 out of 25. Therefore, the probability of not choosing a red ball is 24 out of 25 and the probability of having not a red ball after removing 24 balls is the same. The answer is: $\frac{24}{25}$

Permutations and Combinations

★ **Factorials** are products, indicated by an exclamation mark. For example,
$4! = 4 \times 3 \times 2 \times 1$ (Remember that $0!$ is defined to be equal to 1)

★ **Permutations:** The number of ways to choose a sample of k elements from a set of n distinct objects where order does matter, and replacements are not allowed. For a permutation problem, use this formula:

$$nP_k = \frac{n!}{(n-k)!}$$

★ **Combination:** The number of ways to choose a sample of r elements from a set of n distinct objects where order does not matter, and replacements are not allowed. For a combination problem, use this formula:

$$nC_r = \frac{n!}{r!\,(n-r)!}$$

Examples:

Example 1. How many ways can the first and second place be awarded to 6 people?

Solution: Since the order matters, (the first and second place are different!) we need to use permutation formula where n is 6 and k is 2.
Then: $\frac{n!}{(n-k)!} = \frac{6!}{(6-2)!} = \frac{6!}{4!} = \frac{6\times5\times4!}{4!}$, remove $4!$ from both sides of the fraction. Then: $\frac{6\times5\times4!}{4!} = 6 \times 5 = 30$

Example 2. How many ways can we pick a team of 4 people from a group of 9?

Solution: Since the order doesn't matter, we need to use a combination formula where n is 9 and r is 4.
Then: $\frac{n!}{r!\,(n-r)!} = \frac{9!}{4!\,(9-4)!} = \frac{9!}{4!\,(5)!} = \frac{9\times8\times7\times6\times5!}{4!\,(5)!} = \frac{9\times8\times7\times6}{4\times3\times2\times1} = \frac{3{,}024}{24} = 126$

Function Notation and Evaluation

✰ Functions are mathematical operations that assign unique outputs to given inputs.

✰ Function notation is the way a function is written. It is meant to be a precise way of giving information about the function without a rather lengthy written explanation.

✰ The most popular function notation is $f(x)$ which is read "f of x". Any letter can name a function. for example: $g(x)$, $h(x)$, etc.

✰ To evaluate a function, plug in the input (the given value or expression) for the function's variable (place holder, x).

Examples:

Example 1. Evaluate: $f(x) = 2x + 9$, find $f(5)$

Solution: Substitute x with 5:
Then: $f(x) = 2x + 9 \rightarrow f(5) = 2(5) + 9 \rightarrow f(5) = 19$

Example 2. Evaluate: $w(x) = 5x - 4$, find $w(2)$.

Solution: Substitute x with 2:
Then: $w(x) = 5x - 4 \rightarrow w(2) = 5(2) - 4 = 10 - 4 = 6$

Example 3. Evaluate: $f(x) = 5x^2 + 8$, find $f(-2)$.

Solution: Substitute x with -2:
Then: $f(x) = 5x^2 + 8 \rightarrow f(-2) = 5(-2)^2 + 8 \rightarrow f(-2) = 20 + 8 = 28$

Example 4. Evaluate: $h(x) = 3x^2 - 4$, find $h(3a)$.

Solution: Substitute x with $3a$:
Then: $h(x) = 3x^2 - 4 \rightarrow h(3a) = 3(3a)^2 - 4 \rightarrow h(3a) = 3(9a^2) - 4 = 27a^2 - 4$

Adding and Subtracting Functions

✩ Just like we can add and subtract numbers and expressions, we can add or subtract functions and simplify or evaluate them. The result is a new function.

✩ For two functions $f(x)$ and $g(x)$, we can create two new functions:

$$(f + g)(x) = f(x) + g(x) \text{ and } (f - g)(x) = f(x) - g(x)$$

Examples:

Example 1. $g(x) = 4x - 3$, $f(x) = x + 6$, Find: $(g + f)(x)$

Solution: $(g + f)(x) = g(x) + f(x)$
Then: $(g + f)(x) = (4x - 3) + (x + 6) = 4x - 3 + x + 6 = 5x + 3$

Example 2. $f(x) = 2x - 7$, $g(x) = x - 9$, Find: $(f - g)(x)$

Solution: $(f - g)(x) = f(x) - g(x)$
Then: $(f - g)(x) = (2x - 7) - (x - 9) = 2x - 7 - x + 9 = x + 2$

Example 3. $g(x) = 2x^2 + 6$, $f(x) = x - 3$, Find: $(g + f)(x)$

Solution: $(g + f)(x) = g(x) + f(x)$
Then: $(g + f)(x) = (2x^2 + 6) + (x - 3) = 2x^2 + x + 3$

Example 4. $f(x) = 2x^2 - 1$, $g(x) = 4x + 3$, Find: $(f - g)(2)$

Solution: $(f - g)(x) = f(x) - g(x)$
Then: $(f - g)(x) = (2x^2 - 1) - (4x + 3) = 2x^2 - 1 - 4x - 3 = 2x^2 - 4x - 4$
Substitute x with 2: $(f - g)(2) = 2(2)^2 - 4(2) - 4 = 8 - 8 - 4 = -4$

Multiplying and Dividing Functions

✫ Just like we can multiply and divide numbers and expressions, we can multiply and divide two functions and simplify or evaluate them.

✫ For two functions $f(x)$ and $g(x)$, we can create two new functions:

$$(f.g)(x) = f(x).g(x) \text{ and } \left(\frac{f}{g}\right)(x) = \frac{f(x)}{g(x)}$$

Examples:

Example 1. $g(x) = x + 2$, $f(x) = x + 5$, Find: $(g.f)(x)$

Solution:

$(g.f)(x) = g(x).f(x) = (x + 2)(x + 5) = x^2 + 5x + 2x + 10 = x^2 + 7x + 10$

Example 2. $f(x) = x + 4$, $h(x) = x - 16$, Find: $\left(\frac{f}{h}\right)(x)$

Solution: $\left(\frac{f}{h}\right)(x) = \frac{f(x)}{h(x)} = \frac{x+4}{x-16}$

Example 3. $g(x) = x + 5$, $f(x) = x - 2$, Find: $(g.f)(3)$

Solution: $(g.f)(x) = g(x).f(x) = (x + 5)(x - 2) = x^2 - 2x + 5x - 10$

$$g(x).f(x) = x^2 + 3x - 10$$

Substitute x with 3: $(g.f)(3) = (3)^2 + 3(3) - 10 = 9 + 9 - 10 = 8$

Example 4. $f(x) = 2x + 2$, $h(x) = x - 3$, Find: $\left(\frac{f}{h}\right)(4)$

Solution: $\left(\frac{f}{h}\right)(x) = \frac{f(x)}{h(x)} = \frac{2x+2}{x-3}$

Substitute x with 4: $\left(\frac{f}{h}\right)(4) = \frac{2x+2}{x-3} = \frac{2(4)+2}{4-3} = \frac{10}{1} = 10$

Composition of Functions

★ "Composition of functions" simply means combining two or more functions in a way where the output from one function becomes the input for the next function.

★ The notation used for composition is: $(fog)(x) = f(g(x))$ and is read

"f composed with g of x" or "f of g of x".

Examples:

Example 1. Using $f(x) = x + 5$ and $g(x) = 7x$, find: $(fog)(x)$

Solution: $(fog)(x) = f(g(x))$. Then: $(fog)(x) = f(g(x)) = f(7x)$

Now find $f(7x)$ by substituting x with $7x$ in $f(x)$ function.

Then: $f(x) = x + 5$; $(x \rightarrow 7x) \rightarrow f(7x) = 7x + 5$

Example 2. Using $f(x) = 2x - 3$ and $g(x) = x - 5$, find: $(gof)(3)$

Solution: $(fog)(x) = f(g(x))$. Then: $(gof)(x) = g(f(x)) = g(2x - 3)$,

Now substitute x in $g(x)$ by $(2x - 3)$.

Then: $g(2x - 3) = (2x - 3) - 5 = 2x - 8$

Substitute x with 3: $(gof)(3) = g(f(x)) = 2x - 8 = 2(3) - 8 = -2$

Example 3. Using $f(x) = 3x^2 - 7$ and $g(x) = 2x + 1$, find: $f(g(2))$

Solution: First, find $g(2)$: $g(x) = 2x + 1 \rightarrow g(2) = 2(2) + 1 = 5$

Then: $f(g(2)) = f(5)$. Now, find $f(5)$ by substituting x with 5 in $f(x)$ function.

$f(g(2)) = f(5) = 3(5)^2 - 7 = 3(25) - 7 = 68$

Day 10: Practices

✍ Find the values of the Given Data.

1) 9, 10, 9, 8, 11

2) 6, 8, 1, 4, 7, 6, 10

Mode: _____   Range: _____   Mean: _____   Median: _____

✍ The circle graph below shows all Bob's expenses for last month. Bob spent $675 on his Rent last month.

Bob's last month expenses

3) How much did Bob's total expenses last month? _____

4) How much did Bob spend for his bills last month? _____

5) How much did Bob spend for his car last month? _____

Rent 45%
Foods 10%
Bills 28%
Car 14%
Others 3%

✍ Solve.

6) Bag A contains 9 red marbles and 6 green marbles. Bag B contains 6 black marbles and 9 orange marbles. What is the probability of selecting a red marble at random from bag A? What is the probability of selecting a black marble at random from Bag B?

_____   _____

7) Jason is planning for his vacation. He wants to go to museum, go to the beach, and play volleyball. How many different ways of ordering are there for him? _____

8) In how many ways can a team of 8 basketball players choose a captain and co-captain? _____

9) How many ways can you give 9 balls to your 12 friends? _____

✎ Evaluate each function.

10) $g(n) = 3n + 7$, find $g(3)$

_____

11) $h(x) = 4n - 7$, find $h(5)$

_____

12) $y(n) = 12 - 3n$, find $y(8)$

_____

13) $b(n) = -10 - 5n$, find $b(8)$

_____

14) $g(x) = -7x + 6$, find $g(-3)$

_____

15) $k(n) = -4n + 5$, find $k(-5)$

_____

16) $w(n) = -3n - 6$, find $w(-4)$

_____

17) $z(n) = 14 - 2n$, find $n(3)$

_____

✎ Perform the indicated operation.

18) $f(x) = 2x + 3$

$g(x) = x + 4$

Find $(f - g)(x)$

_____

19) $g(a) = -3a + 2$

$h(a) = a^2 - 4$

Find $(h + g)(3)$

_____

✎ Perform the indicated operation.

20) $g(x) = x - 4$

$f(x) = x + 3$

Find $(g.f)(2)$

_____

21) $f(x) = x + 2$

$h(x) = x - 5$

Find $\left(\frac{f}{h}\right)(-3)$

_____

✎ Using $f(x) = 2x + 5$ and $g(x) = 2x - 3$, find:

22) $g\big(f(2)\big) =$ _____

23) $g\big(f(-2)\big) =$ _____

24) $f\big(f(1)\big) =$ _____

25) $f\big(f(-1)\big) =$ _____

26) $f\big(g(4)\big) =$ _____

27) $f\big(g(-3)\big) =$ _____

Day 10: Answers

1) Mode = the value in the list that appears most often = 9
Range: the difference of the largest value and smallest value. Then:
$11 - 8 = 3$

2) Mean: $\dfrac{sum\ of\ the\ data}{total\ number\ of\ data\ entires} = \dfrac{6+8+1+4+7+6+10}{7} = \dfrac{42}{7} = 6$
Median: is the middle number of a group of numbers arranged in order by size. Write the numbers in order: $1, 4, 6, 7, 8, 10$. Then: Median $= \dfrac{6+7}{2} = 6.5$

3) Bob's rent = \$675

Total expenses → 45% of total expenses = rent →

Total expenses = rent ÷ 0.45 = \$675 ÷ 0.45 = \$1,500

4) Bills = 28% × total expenses = 0.28 × \$1,500 = \$420

5) Car = 14% × total expenses = 0.14 × \$1,500 = 210

6) Probability of pulling out a red marble from bag A $= \dfrac{numbers\ of\ red\ marbles}{total\ of\ marbles} =$
$\dfrac{9}{6+9} = \dfrac{9}{15} = 0.6 = 60\%$
Probability of pulling out a black marble from bag B $=$
$\dfrac{numbers\ of\ black\ marbles}{total\ of\ marbles} = \dfrac{6}{6+9} = \dfrac{6}{15} = 0.4 = 40\%$

7) Jason has 3 choices. Therefore, number of different ways of ordering the events is: $3 \times 2 \times 1 = 6$

8) This is a permutation problem. (order is important) Then: $nP_k = \dfrac{n!}{(n-k)!} \to n =$
$8, k = 2 \to \dfrac{8!}{(8-2)!} = \dfrac{8!}{6!} = \dfrac{8 \times 7 \times 6!}{6!} = 56$

9) This is a combination problem (order doesn't matter) $nC_r = \dfrac{n!}{r!\,(n-r)!} \to$
$n = 12, r = 9 \to nC_r = \dfrac{12!}{9!\,(12-9)!} = \dfrac{12!}{9!\,3!} = \dfrac{12 \times 11 \times 10 \times 9!}{3 \times 2 \times 1 \times 9!} = \dfrac{1,320}{6} = 220$

10) $g(n) = 3n + 7 \to g(3) = 3(3) + 7 = 9 + 7 = 16$

11) $h(x) = 4n - 7 \to h(5) = 4(5) - 7 = 20 - 7 = 13$

12) $y(n) = 12 - 3n \to y(8) = 12 - 3(8) = 12 - 24 = -12$

13) $b(n) = -10 - 5n \to b(8) = -10 - 5(8) = -10 - 40 = -50$

14) $g(x) = -7x + 6 \to g(-3) = -7(-3) + 6 = 21 + 6 = 27$

15) $k(n) = -4n + 5 \to k(-5) = -4(-5) + 5 = 20 + 5 = 25$

16) $w(n) = -3n - 6 \rightarrow w(-4) = -3(-4) - 6 = 12 - 6 = 6$

17) $z(n) = 14 - 2n \rightarrow n(3) = 14 - 2(3) = 14 - 6 = 8$

18) $(f - g)(x) = f(x) - g(x) = 2x + 3 - (x + 4) = 2x + 3 - x - 4 = x - 1$

19) $(h + g)(3) = h(a) + g(a) = a^2 - 4 - 3a + 2 = a^2 - 3a - 2 = (3)^2 - 3(3) - 2 =$
$9 - 9 - 2 = -2$

20) $(g.f)(2) = f(x) \times g(x) = (x - 4) \times (x + 3) = (x \times x) + (x \times 3) + (-4 \times x) +$
$(-4 \times 3) = x^2 + 3x - 4x - 12 = x^2 - x - 12 = 2^2 - 2 - 12 = 4 - 2 - 12 = -10$

21) $\left(\frac{f}{h}\right)(-3) = \frac{f(x)}{h(x)} = \frac{x+2}{x-5} = \frac{(-3)+2}{(-3)-5} = \frac{-3+2}{-3-5} = \frac{-1}{-8} = \frac{1}{8}$

22) First, find $f(2)$: $f(x) = 2x + 5 \rightarrow f(2) = 2(2) + 5 = 9$

Then: $g(f(2)) = g(9)$. Now, find $g(9)$ by substituting x with 9 in $g(x)$

function. $g(f(2)) = g(9) = 2(9) - 3 = 18 - 3 = 15$

23) First, find $f(-2)$: $f(x) = 2x + 5 \rightarrow f(-2) = 2(-2) + 5 = -4 + 5 = 1$

Then: $g(f(-2)) = g(1)$. Now, find $g(1)$ by substituting x with 1 in $g(x)$

function. $g(f(-2)) = g(1) = 2(1) - 3 = 2 - 3 = -1$

24) First, find $f(1)$: $f(x) = 2x + 5 \rightarrow f(1) = 2(1) + 5 = 2 + 5 = 7$

Then: $f(f(1)) = f(7)$. Now, find $f(7)$ by substituting x with 7 in $f(x)$

function. $f(f(1)) = f(7) = 2(7) + 5 = 14 + 5 = 19$

25) First, find $f(-1)$: $f(x) = 2x + 5 \rightarrow f(-1) = 2(-1) + 5 = -2 + 5 = 3$

Then: $f(f(-1)) = f(3)$. Now, find $f(3)$ by substituting x with 3 in $f(x)$

function. $f(g(-1)) = f(3) = 2(3) + 5 = 6 + 5 = 11$

26) First, find $g(4)$: $g(x) = 2x - 3 \rightarrow g(4) = 2(4) - 3 = 8 - 3 = 5$

Then: $f(g(4)) = f(5)$. Now, find $f(5)$ by substituting x with 5 in $f(x)$

function. $f(g(4)) = f(5) = 2(5) + 5 = 10 + 5 = 15$

27) First, find $g(-3)$: $g(x) = 2x - 3 \rightarrow g(-3) = 2(-3) - 3 = -6 - 3 = -9$

Then: $f(g(-3)) = f(-9)$. Now, find $f(-9)$ by substituting x with -9 in

$f(x)$. function. $f(g(-3)) = f(-9) = 2(-9) + 5 = -18 + 5 = -13$

Time to Test

Time to refine your skill with a practice examination

In this section, there are 2 complete GED Mathematical Reasoning Tests. Take these tests to see what score you'll be able to receive on a real GED test. After you've finished, score your test using the answer key.

Before You Start

- ❖ You'll need a pencil and a calculator to take the test.
- ❖ There are two types of questions:
- ❖ Multiple choice questions: for each of these questions, there are four or more possible answers. Choose which one is best.
- ❖ Grid-ins questions: for these questions, write your answer in the box provided.
- ❖ It's okay to guess. You won't lose any points if you're wrong.
- ❖ The GED Mathematical Reasoning test contains a formula sheet, which displays formulas relating to geometric measurement and certain algebra concepts. Formulas are provided to test-takers so that they may focus on application, rather than the memorization, of formulas.
- ❖ After you've finished the test, review the answer key to see where you went wrong and what areas you need to improve.

Good luck!

GED Mathematical Reasoning Practice Test 1

2023

Two Parts

Total number of questions: 46

Part 1 (Non-Calculator): 5 questions

Part 2 (Calculator): 41 questions

Total time for two parts: <u>115 Minutes</u>

GED Test Mathematics Formula Sheet

Area of a:

Parallelogram

$$A = bh$$

Trapezoid

$$A = \frac{1}{2}h(b_1 + b_2)$$

Surface Area and Volume of a:

Rectangular/Right Prism

$$SA = ph + 2B \qquad V = Bh$$

Cylinder

$$SA = 2\pi rh + 2\pi r^2 \qquad V = \pi r^2 h$$

Pyramid

$$SA = \frac{1}{2}ps + B \qquad V = \frac{1}{3}Bh$$

Cone

$$SA = \pi r + \pi r^2 \qquad V = \frac{1}{3}\pi r^2 h$$

Sphere

$$SA = 4\pi r^2 \qquad V = \frac{4}{3}\pi r^3$$

(p = perimeter of base B; $\pi = 3.14$)

Algebra

Slope of a line

$$m = \frac{y_2 - y_1}{x_2 - x_1}$$

Slope-intercept form of the equation of a line

$$y = mx + b$$

Point-slope form of the Equation of a line

$$y - y_1 = m(x - x_1)$$

Standard form of a Quadratic equation

$$y = ax^2 + bx + c$$

Quadratic formula

$$x = \frac{-b \pm \sqrt{b^2 - 4ac}}{2a}$$

Pythagorean theorem

$$a^2 + b^2 = c^2$$

Simple interest

$$I = prt$$
(I = interest, p = principal, r = rate, t = time)

GED Mathematical Reasoning Practice Test 1 Part 1 (Non-Calculator)

5 questions

Total time for two parts (Non-Calculator and Calculator parts): 115 Minutes

You may NOT use a calculator on this part.

1) Which of the following is the same as: 0.000 000 000 000 042 121?

    ☐A. 4.2121×10^{14} ☐B. 4.2121×10^{-14}

    ☐C. $42,121 \times 10^{-10}$ ☐D. 42.121×10^{-13}

2) 5 less than twice a positive integer is 83. What is the integer?

    ☐A.39   ☐B.41

    ☐C.42   ☐D.44

3) A shirt costing $200 is discounted 15%. After a month, the shirt is discounted another 15%. Which of the following expressions can be used to find the selling price of the shirt?

    ☐A. $(200)(0.70)$ ☐B. $(200) - 200(0.30)$

    ☐C. $(200)(0.15) - (200)(0.15)$ ☐D. $(200)(0.85)(0.85)$

4) Which of the following points lies on the line $2x + 4y = 10$

    ☐A. $(2, 1)$ ☐B. $(-1, 3)$

    ☐C. $(-2, 2)$ ☐D. $(2, 2)$

5) What is the value of the expression? $5 + 8 \times (-2) - [4 + 22 \times 5] \div 6$

    Write your answer in the box below.

GED Mathematical Reasoning Practice Test 1 Part 2 (Calculator)

41 questions
Total time for two parts (Non-Calculator, and Calculator parts): 115 Minutes

You may use a calculator on this part.

6) A student gets an 85% on a test with 40 questions. How many answers did the student solve correctly?

   ☐ A. 25   ☐ B. 28

   ☐ C. 34   ☐ D. 36

7) The width of a box is one third of its length. The height of the box is one third of its width. If the length of the box is 27 cm, what is the volume of the box?

   ☐ A. 81 cm^3 ☐ B. 162 cm^3

   ☐ C. 243 cm^3 ☐ D. 729 cm^3

8) If 60% of A is 30% of B, then B is what percent of A?

   ☐ A. 3%   ☐ B. 30%

   ☐ C. 200%   ☐ D. 300%

9) How many possible outfit combinations come from six shirts, three slacks, and five ties?

Write your answer in the box below.

```
┌─────────────────────────┐
│                         │
└─────────────────────────┘
```

10) A ladder leans against a wall forming a 60° angle between the ground and the ladder. If the bottom of the ladder is 30 feet away from the wall, how long is the ladder?

   ☐ A. 30 $feet$ ☐ B. 40 $feet$

   ☐ C. 50 $feet$ ☐ D. 60 $feet$

11) When a number is subtracted from 24 and the difference is divided by that number, the result is 3. What is the value of the number?

   ☐ A. 2   ☐ B. 4

   ☐ C. 6   ☐ D. 12

12) An angle is equal to one fifth of its supplement. What is the measure of that angle in degrees?

☐A. 20°   ☐B. 30°

☐ C. 45°   ☐D. 60°

13) John traveled 150 km in 6 hours and Alice traveled 180 km in 4 hours. What is the ratio of the average speed of John to average speed of Alice?

☐A. 3: 2   ☐B. 2: 3

☐C. 5: 9   ☐D. 5: 6

14) If 40% of a class are girls, and 25% of girls play tennis, what percent of the class play tennis?

☐A. 10%   ☐B. 15%

☐C. 20%   ☐D. 40%

15) What is the value of y in the following system of equation?

$$3x - 4y = -40$$

$$-x + 2y = 10$$

Write your answer in the box below.

☐

16) In five successive hours, a car travels 40 km, 45 km, 50 km, 35 km and 55 km. In the next five hours, it travels with an average speed of 50 km per $hour$. Find the total distance the car traveled in 10 hours.

☐A. 425 km ☐B. 450 km

☐C. 475 km ☐D. 500 km

17) How long does a 420-miles trip take moving at 50 miles per hour (mph)?

☐A. 4 $hours$ ☐B. 6 $hours$ and 24 $minutes$
☐C. 8 $hours$ and 24 $minutes$ ☐D. 8 $hours$ and 30 $minutes$

18) In a bag there are only red marbles and blue marbles. The ratio of red marbles to blue marbles is $2:5$. Which of the following could be the total number of marbles in the bag? (Select one or more answer choices)

   ☐A. 324   ☐C. 826   ☐E. 662

   ☐ B. 688   ☐D. 596

19) Which of the following points lies on the line $3x + 2y = 11$? (Select one or more answer choices)

   ☐A. $(-1, 3)$ ☐C. $(-1, 7)$ ☐E. $(0, 2)$

   ☐ B. $(2, 3)$ ☐D. $(5, -2)$

20) Right triangle ABC has two legs of lengths $6 \, cm$ (AB) and $8 \, cm$ (AC). What is the length of the third side (BC)?

   ☐ A. $4 \, cm$ ☐ B. $6 \, cm$

   ☐ C. $8 \, cm$ ☐ D. $10 \, cm$

21) The ratio of boys to girls in a school is $2:3$. If there are 600 students in a school, how many boys are in the school.
Write your answer in the box below.

        ┌──────────────────────┐
        │   │
        └──────────────────────┘

22) 25 is What percent of 20?

   ☐A. 20%   ☐B. 25%

   ☐C. 125%   ☐D. 150%

23) The perimeter of the trapezoid below is 64. What is its area?

Write your answer in the box below.

        ┌──────────────────────┐
        │   │
        └──────────────────────┘

18

12   14

24) Two third of 18 is equal to $\frac{2}{5}$ of what number?

    ☐A. 12   ☐B. 20

    ☐C. 30   ☐D. 60

25) The marked price of a computer is D dollar. Its price decreased by 20% in January and later increased by 10% in February. What is the final price of the computer in D dollar?

    ☐A. 0.80 D ☐B. 0.88 D

    ☐C. 0.90 D ☐D. 1.20 D

26) The area of a circle is $64\,\pi$. What is the circumference of the circle?

    ☐A. $8\,\pi$ ☐B. $16\,\pi$

    ☐C. $32\,\pi$ ☐D. $64\,\pi$

27) A $40 shirt now selling for $28 is discounted by what percent?

    ☐A. 20%   ☐B. 30%

    ☐C. 40%   ☐D. 60%

28) In 1999, the average worker's income increased $2,000 per year starting from $24,000 annual salary. Which equation represents income greater than average? (I = income),

   x = number of years after 1999)

    ☐A. $I > 2,000\,x + 24,000$ ☐B. $I > -2,000\,x + 24,000$

    ☐C. $I < -2000\,x + 24,000$ ☐D. $I < 2,000\,x - 24,000$

29) From last year, the price of gasoline has increased from $1.25 per gallon to $1.75 per gallon. The new price is what percent of the original price?

    ☐A. 72%   ☐B. 120%

    ☐C. 140%   ☐D. 160%

30) A boat sails 40 miles south and then 30 miles east. How far is the boat from its start point?

   □A. 45 *miles*   □B. 50 *miles*

   □C. 60 *miles*   □D. 70 *miles*

31) Which of the following could be the product of two consecutive prime numbers?

   □A. 2   □B. 10

   □C. 14   □D. 15

32) Jason purchased a laptop for $529.72. The laptop is regularly priced at $646.00. What was the percent discount Jason received on the laptop?

   □A. 12%   □B. 18%

   □C. 20%   □D. 25%

33) The score of Emma was half as that of Ava and the score of Mia was twice that of Ava. If the score of Mia was 40, what is the score of Emma?

   □A. 5   □B. 10

   □C. 20   □D. 40

34) A bag contains 18 balls: two green, five black, eight blue, a brown, a red and one white. If 17 balls are removed from the bag at random, what is the probability that a brown ball has been removed?

   □A. $\frac{1}{9}$ □B. $\frac{1}{6}$

   □C. $\frac{16}{17}$ □D. $\frac{17}{18}$

35) The average of five consecutive numbers is 38. What is the smallest number?

   □A. 38   □B. 36
   □C. 34   □D. 12

36) How many tiles of 8 cm^2 is needed to cover a floor of dimension 8 cm by 24 cm?

- [ ] A. 6
- [ ] B. 12
- [ ] C. 18
- [ ] D. 24

37) A rope weighs 600 grams per meter of length. What is the weight in kilograms of 12.2 meters of this rope? (1 $kilograms$ = 1,000 $grams$)

- [ ] A. 0.0732
- [ ] B. 0.732
- [ ] C. 7.32
- [ ] D. 7.320

38) A chemical solution contains 4% alcohol. If there is 32 ml of alcohol, what is the volume of the solution?

- [ ] A. 240 ml
- [ ] B. 480 ml
- [ ] C. 800 ml
- [ ] D. 1.200 ml

39) The average weight of 23 girls in a class is 60 kg and the average weight of 32 boys in the same class is 62 kg. What is the average weight of all the 50 students in that class?

- [ ] A. 60
- [ ] B. 61.16
- [ ] C. 61.68
- [ ] D. 62.90

40) The price of a laptop is decreased by 20% to $360. What is its original price?

- [ ] A. 320
- [ ] B. 380
- [ ] C. 400
- [ ] D. 450

41) What is the median of these numbers? 3, 10, 13, 8, 15, 19, 5

- [ ] A. 8
- [ ] B. 10
- [ ] C. 13
- [ ] D. 15

42) The radius of the following cylinder is 6 inches and its height is 12 inches. What is the surface area of the cylinder in square inches?

Write your answer in the box below. (π equals 3.14)

```
┌──────────────────────┐
│                      │
│                      │
└──────────────────────┘
```

43) The average of $13, 15, 20$ and x is 15. What is the value of x?

Write your answer in the box below.

```
┌──────────────────────┐
│                      │
│                      │
└──────────────────────┘
```

44) The price of a sofa is decreased by 25% to $420. What was its original price?

☐A. $480   ☐B. $520
☐C. $560   ☐D. $600

45) In the xy-plane, the point $(1, 2)$ and $(-1, 6)$ are on line A. Which of the following points could also be on line A? (Select one or more answer choices)

☐A. $(-1, 2)$ ☐C. $(3, 4)$ ☐E. $(6, -8)$
☐ B. $(5, 7)$ ☐D. $(3, -2)$

46) A bank is offering 4.5% simple interest on a savings account. If you deposit $9,000, how much interest will you earn in five years?

☐A. $405   ☐B. $720
☐C. $2,025   ☐D. $3,600

End of GED Mathematical Reasoning Practice Test 1.

GED Mathematical Reasoning Practice Test 2

2023

Two Parts

Total number of questions: 46

Part 1 (Non-Calculator): 5 questions

Part 2 (Calculator): 41 questions

Total time for two parts: <u>115 Minutes</u>

GED Test Mathematics Formula Sheet

Area of a:

Parallelogram

$$A = bh$$

Trapezoid

$$A = \frac{1}{2}h(b_1 + b_2)$$

Surface Area and Volume of a:

Rectangular/Right Prism

$$SA = ph + 2B \qquad V = Bh$$

Cylinder

$$SA = 2\pi rh + 2\pi r^2 \qquad V = \pi r^2 h$$

Pyramid

$$SA = \frac{1}{2}ps + B \qquad V = \frac{1}{3}Bh$$

Cone

$$SA = \pi r + \pi r^2 \qquad V = \frac{1}{3}\pi r^2 h$$

Sphere

$$SA = 4\pi r^2 \qquad V = \frac{4}{3}\pi r^3$$

(p = perimeter of base B; π = 3.14)

Algebra

Slope of a line

$$m = \frac{y_2 - y_1}{x_2 - x_1}$$

Slope-intercept form of the equation of a line

$$y = mx + b$$

Point-slope form of the Equation of a line

$$y - y_1 = m(x - x_1)$$

Standard form of a Quadratic equation

$$y = ax^2 + bx + c$$

Quadratic formula

$$x = \frac{-b \pm \sqrt{b^2 - 4ac}}{2a}$$

Pythagorean theorem

$$a^2 + b^2 = c^2$$

Simple interest

$$I = prt$$

(I = interest, p = principal, r = rate, t = time)

GED Mathematical Reasoning Practice Test 2 Part 1 (Non-Calculator)

5 questions
Total time for two parts (Non-Calculator, and Calculator parts): 115 Minutes

You may NOT use a calculator on this part.

1) If $3x - 5 = 8.5$, what is the value of $6x + 3$?

    □A. 13   □B. 15.5

    □C. 20.5   □D. 30

2) What is the area of an isosceles right triangle that has one leg that measures $8\ cm$?

    □A. $6\ cm^2$ □B. $12\ cm^2$

    □C. $18\ cm^2$ □D. $32\ cm^2$

3) A shirt costing $600 is discounted 25%. After a month, the shirt is discounted another 15%. Which of the following expressions can be used to find the selling price of the shirt?

    □A. $(600)(0.60)$ □B. $(600) - 600\ (0.40)$

    □C. $(600)(0.25) - (200)(0.15)$ □D. $(600)(0.75)(0.85)$

4) Which of the following points lies on the line with equation $3x + 5y = 11$?

    □A. $(2, 1)$ □B. $(-1, 2)$

    □C. $(-2, 2)$ □D. $(2, 2)$

5) What is the value of expression? $-15 + 6 \times (-5) - [4 + 22 \times (-4)] \div 2 = ?$

Write your answer in the box below.

GED Mathematical Reasoning Practice Test 2 Part 2 (Calculator)

41 questions
Total time for two parts (Non-Calculator, and Calculator parts): 115 Minutes

You may use a calculator on this part.

6) The average of five consecutive numbers is 40. What is the smallest number?

   ☐A. 38   ☐B. 36
   ☐C. 34   ☐D. 12

7) How many tiles of $8 \ cm^2$ is needed to cover a floor of dimension $7 \ cm$ by $24 \ cm$?

   ☐A. 6   ☐B. 12
   ☐C. 21   ☐D. 24

8) A rope weighs 600 grams per meter of length. What is the weight in kilograms of 15.2 meters of this rope? (1 $kilograms \ = 1,000 \ grams$)

   ☐A. 0.0912   ☐B. 0.912
   ☐C. 9.12   ☐D. 91.20

9) A chemical solution contains 6% alcohol. If there is $24 \ ml$ of alcohol, what is the volume of the solution?

   ☐A. $240 \ ml$ ☐B. $400 \ ml$
   ☐C. $600 \ ml$ ☐D. $1200 \ ml$

10) The average weight of 18 girls in a class is $60 \ kg$ and the average weight of 32 boys in the same class is $62 \ kg$. What is the average weight of all the 50 students in that class?

   ☐A. 60   ☐B. 61.28
   ☐C. 61.68   ☐D. 62.90

11) The price of a laptop is decreased by 10% to $360. What is its original price?

   ☐A. $320   ☐B. $380
   ☐C. $400   ☐D. $450

12) What is the median of these numbers? $4, 9, 13, 8, 15, 18, 5$

   ☐A. 8   ☐B. 9
   ☐C. 13   ☐D. 15

13) The radius of a cylinder is 8 inches and its height is 16 inches. What is the surface area of the cylinder in square inches?

Write your answer in the box below. (π equals 3.14)

14) In 1.999, the average worker's income increased \$2,000 per year starting from \$27,000 annual salary. Which equation represents income greater than average? (I = income, x = number of years after 1.999)

☐A. $I > 2,000\,x + 27,000$ ☐B. $I > -\,2,000\,x + 27,000$

☐C. $I < -2,000\,x + 27,000$ ☐D. $I < 2,000\,x - 27,000$

15) What is the value of y in the following system of equation?

$$3x - 4y = -20$$
$$-x + 2y = 10$$

Write your answer in the box below.

16) What is the area of a square whose diagonal is 6 meters?

☐ A. $20\ m^2$ ☐B. $18\ m^2$

☐ C. $12\ m^2$ ☐D. $10\ m^2$

17) The width of a box is one third of its length. The height of the box is half of its width. If the length of the box is 24 cm, what is the volume of the box?

☐A. $81\ cm^3$ ☐ B. $162\ cm^3$

☐C. $243\ cm^3$ ☐ D. $768\ cm^3$

18) If 60% of A is 20% of B, then B is what percent of A?

☐A. 3% ☐B. 30%

☐ C. 200% ☐D. 300%

19) How many possible outfit combinations come from six shirts, three slacks, and six ties?

Write your answer in the box below.

20) A bank is offering 2.5% simple interest on a savings account. If you deposit $8,000, how much interest will you earn in five years?

☐A. $360 ☐B. $720

☐C. $1,000 ☐D. $3,600

21) What is the value of 6^5 ?

Write your answer in the box below.

22) 15 is What percent of 20?

☐A. 20% ☐B. 75%

☐C. 125% ☐D. 150%

23) The perimeter of the trapezoid below is 50. What is its area?

Write your answer in the box below.

24) In five successive hours, a car travels $40\ km$, $45\ km$, $50\ km$, $35\ km$ and $55\ km$. In the next five hours, it travels with an average speed of $45\ km\ per\ hour$. Find the total distance the car traveled in $10\ hours$.

☐A. $425\ km$ ☐B. $450\ km$

☐C. $475\ km$ ☐D. $500\ km$

25) How long does a $420-miles$ trip take moving at $60\ miles\ per\ hour\ (mph)$?

☐A. $4\ hours$ ☐B. $7\ hours$

☐C. $7\ hours$ and $24\ minutes$ ☐D. $8\ hours$ and $10\ minutes$

26) Which of the following points lies on the line $4x + 6y = 20$?

☐A. $(2, 1)$ ☐B. $(-1, 3)$

☐C. $(-2, 2)$ ☐D. $(2, 2)$

27) Two third of 15 is equal to $\frac{2}{5}$ of what number?

☐A. 12   ☐B. 20

☐C. 25   ☐D. 60

28) The marked price of a computer is D dollar. Its price decreased by 20% in January and later increased by 15% in February. What is the final price of the computer in D dollar?

☐A. $0.80\ D$ ☐B. $0.88\ D$

☐C. $0.92\ D$ ☐D. 1.20

29) A $45 shirt now selling for $28 is discounted by about what percent?

☐A. 20%   ☐B. 37.7%

☐C. 40%   ☐D. 60%

30) Which of the following could be the product of two consecutive prime numbers? (Select one or more answer choices)

☐A. 2   ☐B. 10

☐C. 14   ☐D. 15

☐E. 35

31) The ratio of boys to girls in a school is $2:3$. If there are 400 students in a school, how many boys are in the school.

Write your answer in the box below.

```
┌──────────────────────────┐
│                          │
│                          │
└──────────────────────────┘
```

32) Sophia purchased a sofa for $537.50. The sofa is regularly priced at $625. What was the percent discount Sophia received on the sofa?

☐A. 12%   ☐B. 14%

☐C. 20%   ☐D. 25%

33) The score of Emma was half as that of Ava and the score of Mia was twice that of Ava. If the score of Mia was 60, what is the score of Emma?

☐A. 12   ☐B. 15

☐C. 20   ☐D. 30

34) A bag contains 21 balls: two green, six black, eight blue, two brown, two red and one white. If 20 balls are removed from the bag at random, what is the probability that a white ball has been removed?

☐A. $\frac{1}{9}$ ☐B. $\frac{1}{6}$

☐C. $\frac{4}{5}$ ☐D. $\frac{20}{21}$

35) A taxi driver earns $8 per 1-hour work. If he works 10 hours a day and in 1 hour he uses 2-liters petrol with price $1 for 1-liter. How much money does he earn in one day?

☐A. $90   ☐B. $88

☐C. $70   ☐D. $60

36) The average of $13, 15, 20$ and x is 25. What is the value of x?

Write your answer in the box below.

```
┌──────────────────────────┐
│                          │
│                          │
└──────────────────────────┘
```

37) The price of a sofa is decreased by 15% to $476. What was its original price?

☐A. $480   ☐B. $520

☐C. $560   ☐D. $600

38) When a number is subtracted from 28 and the difference is divided by that number, the result is 3. What is the value of the number?

☐A. 2   ☐B. 4

☐C. 7   ☐D. 12

39) An angle is equal to one fourth of its supplement. What is the measure of that angle?

☐A.18   ☐B. 24

☐ C. 36   ☐D. 45

40) John traveled 150 km in 6 hours and Alice traveled 160 km in 4 hours. What is the ratio of the average speed of John to average speed of Alice?

☐A. 3 : 2   ☐B. 2 : 3

☐C. 5 : 8   ☐D. 5 : 6

41) Right triangle ABC has two legs of lengths 5 cm (AB) and 12 cm (AC). What is the length of the third side (BC)?

☐ A. 6 cm ☐ B. 8 cm

☐ C. 13 cm ☐ D. 15 cm

42) If 75% of a class are girls, and $\frac{1}{3}$ of girls take drawing class this semester, what percent of the class are girls who take drawing class this semester?

☐A. 25%   ☐B. 28%

☐C. 35%   ☐D. 37.5%

43) The area of a circle is less than 49π. Which of the following can be the circumference of the circle? (Select one or more answer choices)

☐A. 8π ☐B. 12π

☐C. 14π ☐D. 32π

☐E. 49π

44) If $2y + 6 < 30$, then y could be equal to? (Select one or more answer choices)

☐A. 15   ☐B. 14

☐C. 12   ☐D. 8

☐E. -12

45) From last year, the price of a table has increased from $125.00 to $185.00. The new price is what percent of the original price?

☐A. 72%   ☐B. 120%

☐C. 148%   ☐D. 160%

46) A boat sails 80 *miles* south and then 150 *miles* east. How far is the boat from its start point?

☐A. 160 *miles*   ☐B. 170 *miles*

☐C. 200 *miles*   ☐D. 230 *miles*

End of GED Mathematical Reasoning Practice Test 2.

GED Mathematical Reasoning Practice Tests Answer Keys

Now, it's time to review your results to see where you went wrong and what areas you need to improve.

GED Math Practice Test 1

1	B	21	240	41	B
2	D	22	C	42	678.24
3	D	23	130	43	12
4	B	24	C	44	C
5	−30	25	B	45	D, E
6	C	26	B	46	C
7	D	27	B		
8	C	28	A		
9	90	29	C		
10	D	30	B		
11	C	31	D		
12	B	32	B		
13	C	33	B		
14	A	34	D		
15	−5	35	B		
16	C	36	D		
17	C	37	C		
18	C, E	38	C		
19	C, D	39	B		
20	D	40	D		

GED Math Practice Test 2

1	D	**21**	7,776	**41**	C
2	D	**22**	B	**42**	A
3	D	**23**	78	**43**	A, B
4	A	**24**	B	**44**	D, E
5	−3	**25**	B	**45**	C
6	A	**26**	D	**46**	B
7	C	**27**	C		
8	C	**28**	C		
9	B	**29**	B		
10	B	**30**	D, E		
11	C	**31**	160		
12	B	**32**	B		
13	1,205.76	**33**	B		
14	A	**34**	D		
15	5	**35**	D		
16	B	**36**	52		
17	D	**37**	C		
18	D	**38**	C		
19	108	**39**	C		
20	C	**40**	C		

How to score your tests

Each GED area test is scored on a scale of 100 - 200 points. To pass the GED, you must earn at least 145 on each of the four subject tests, for a total of at least 580 points (out of a possible 800).

Each subject test should be passed individually. It means that you must get 145 on each section of the test. If you failed one subject test but did well enough on another to get a total score of 580, that's still not a passing score.

There are four possible scores that you can receive on the GED Test:

Not Passing: This indicates that your score is lower than 145 on any of the four tests. If you do not pass, you can reschedule up to two times a year to retake any or all subjects of the GED test.

Passing Score/High School Equivalency: This score indicates that your score is between 145-164. Remember that points on one subject of the test do not carry over to the other subjects.

College Ready: This indicates that your score is between 165-175, demonstrating career and college readiness. A College Ready score shows that you may not need placement testing or remediation before beginning a college degree program.

College Ready + Credit: This indicates that your score is 175 or higher. This shows that you've already mastered some skills that would be taught in college courses. Depending on a school's policy, this can translate to some college credits–saving you time and money during your college education.

There are approximately 46 questions on GED Mathematical Reasoning. Similar to other subject areas, you will need a minimum score of 145 to pass the Mathematical Reasoning Test. There are 49 raw score points on the GED math test. The raw points correspond with correct answers. Most questions have one answer; therefore, they only have one point. There is more than one point for questions that have more than one answer. You'll get a raw score out of the 49 possible points. This will then be converted into your scaled score out of 200. Approximately, you need to get 32 out of 49 raw score to pass the Mathematical Reasoning section.

To score your GED Mathematical Reasoning practice tests, first find your raw score.

There were 46 questions on each GED Mathematical Reasoning practice test. All questions have one point except following questions that have 2 points:

GED Mathematical Reasoning practice test 1:

Question 18: Two points

Question 19: Two points

Question 45: Two points

GED Mathematical Reasoning practice test 2:

Question 30: Two points

Question 43: Two points

Question 44: Two points

Use the following table to convert GED Mathematical Reasoning raw score to scaled score.

GED Mathematical Reasoning raw score to scaled score	
Raw Scores	Scaled Scores
Below 32 *(not passing)*	*Below* 145
32 − 36	145 − 164
37 − 40	165 − 175
Above 40	*Above* 175

GED Mathematical Reasoning Practice Tests Answers and Explanations

GED Mathematical Reasoning Practice Test 1 Answers and Explanations

1) Choice B is correct

In scientific notation all numbers are written in the form of: $m \times 10^n$, where m is between 1 and 10. To find an equivalent value of 0.000 000 000 000 042 121, move the decimal point to the right so that you have a number that is between 1 and 10. Then: 4.2121

Now, determine how many places the decimal moved in step 1, then put it as the power of 10.

We moved the decimal point 14 places. Then: 10^{-14} →When the decimal moved to the right, the exponent is negative. Then:

0.000 000 000 000 042 121 $= 4.2121 \times 10^{-14}$

2) Choice D is correct

Let x be the integer. Then: $2x - 5 = 83$. Add 5 both sides: $2x = 88$, Divide both sides by 2:

$$x = 44$$

3) Choice D is correct

To find the discount, multiply the number by ($100\% - rate\ of\ discount$). Therefore, for the first discount we get: $(200)(100\% - 15\%) = (200)(0.85) = 170$

For the next 15% discount: $(200)(0.85)(0.85)$

4) Choice B is correct

Plug in each pair of number in the equation:

A. $(2, 1)$: $2(2) + 4(1) = 8$
B. $(-1, 3)$: $2(-1) + 4(3) = 10$
C. $(-2, 2)$: $2(-2) + 4(2) = 4$
D. $(2, 2)$: $2(2) + 4(2) = 12$

Only choice B is correct.

5) The answer is: -30

Use PEMDAS (order of operation):
$$5 + 8 \times (-2) - [4 + 22 \times 5] \div 6 = 5 + 8 \times (-2) - [4 + 110] \div 6$$
$$= 5 + 8 \times (-2) - [114] \div 6 = 5 + (-16) - 19 = 5 + (-16) - 19$$
$$= -11 - 19 = -30$$

6) Choice C is correct

$85\%\ of\ 40 = 0.85 \times 40 = 34$. So, the student solves 34 questions correctly.

7) Choice D is correct

If the length of the box is 27, then the width of the box is one third of it, 9, and the height of the box is 3 (one third of the width). The volume of the box is: $V = lwh = (27)(9)(3) = 729$

8) Choice C is correct

Write the equation and solve for B: $0.60\,A = 0.30\,B$, divide both sides by 0.30, then:

$\frac{0.60}{0.30} A = B$, therefore: $B = 2\,A$, and B is 2 times of A or it's 200% of A.

9) The answer is 90.

To find the number of possible outfit combinations, multiply number of options for each factor:

$6 \times 3 \times 5 = 90$

10) Choice D is correct

The relationship among all sides of special right triangle $30° - 60° - 90°$ is provided in this triangle:

In this triangle, the opposite side of 30° angle is half of the hypotenuse.

Draw the shape for this question:

The ladder is the hypotenuse. Therefore, the ladder is 60 ft.

11) Choice C is correct

Let x be the number. Write the equation and solve for x. $(24 - x) \div x = 3$. Multiply both sides by x. $(24 - x) = 3x$, then add x both sides. $24 = 4x$, now divide both sides by 4. $x = 6$

12) Choice B is correct

The sum of supplement angles is 180. Let x be that angle. Therefore, $x + 5x = 180$. $6x = 180$, divide both sides by 6: $x = 30$

13) Choice C is correct

The average speed of john is: $150 \div 6 = 25\,km$, The average speed of Alice is: $180 \div 4 = 45\,km$. Write the ratio and simplify. $25 : 45 \Rightarrow 5 : 9$

14) Choice A is correct

The percent of girls playing tennis is: $40\% \times 25\% = 0.40 \times 0.25 = 0.10 = 10\%$

15) The answer is −5.

Solving Systems of Equations by Elimination

$3x - 4y = -40$
$\underline{-x + 2y = 10}$ Multiply the second equation by 3, then add it to the first

equation.

$\begin{matrix} 3x - 4y = -40 \\ \underline{3(-x + 2y = 10)} \end{matrix} \Rightarrow \begin{matrix} 3x - 4y = -40 \\ \underline{-3x + 6y = 30)} \end{matrix} \Rightarrow 2y = -10 \Rightarrow y = -5$

16) Choice C is correct

Add the first 5 numbers. $40 + 45 + 50 + 35 + 55 = 225$. To find the distance traveled in the next 5 hours, multiply the average by number of hours. $Distance = Average \times Rate = 50 \times 5 = 250$. Add both numbers. $250 + 225 = 475$

17) Choice C is correct

Use distance formula: $Distance = Rate \times time \Rightarrow 420 = 50 \times T$, divide both sides by 50. $420 \div 50 = T \Rightarrow T = 8.4 \ hours$.

Change hours to minutes for the decimal part. $0.4 \ hours = 0.4 \times 60 = 24 \ minutes$.

18) Choices C and E are correct

(If you selected 3 choices and 2 of them are correct, then you get one point. If you answered 2 or 3 choices and one of them is correct, you receive one point. If you selected more than 3 choices, you won't get any point for this question.) The ratio of red marbles to blue marbles is $2:5$. Therefore, total number of marbles must be divisible by 7: $2 + 5 = 7$. Let's review the choices:

☐A. 324: $324 \div 7 = 46.28 \dots$

☐B. 688: $688 \div 7 = 98.28 \dots$

☐C. 826 $826 \div 7 = 118$

☐ D. 596 $596 \div 7 = 85.14 \dots$

☐ E. 658 $658 \div 7 = 94$

Only choices C and E when divided by 7 result a whole number.

19) Choices C and D are correct

(If you selected 3 choices and 2 of them are correct, then you get one point. If you answered 2 or 3 choices and one of them is correct, you receive one point. If you selected more than 3 choices, you won't get any point for this question.)
$3x + 2y = 11$. Plug in the values of x and y from choices provided. Then:

A. $(-1, 3) \rightarrow x + 2y = 11 \rightarrow 3(-1) + 2(3) = 11 \rightarrow -3 + 6 = 11 \rightarrow$ NOT true!

B. $(2, 3) \rightarrow 3x + 2y = 11 \rightarrow 3(2) + 2(3) = 11 \rightarrow 6 + 6 = 11 \rightarrow$ NOT true!

C. $(-1, 7) \rightarrow 3x + 2y = 11 \rightarrow 3(-1) + 2(7) = 11 \rightarrow -3 + 14 = 11 \rightarrow$ Bingo!

D. $(5, -2) \rightarrow 3x + 2y = 11 \rightarrow 3(5) + 2(-2) = 11 \rightarrow 15 - 4 = 11 \rightarrow$ Yes!

E. $(0, 2) \rightarrow 3x + 2y = 11 \rightarrow 3(0) + 2(2) = 11 \rightarrow 0 + 4 = 11 \rightarrow$ ( )( )Nope!

20) Choice D is correct

Use Pythagorean Theorem: $a^2 + b^2 = c^2$, $6^2 + 8^2 = c^2 \rightarrow 100 = c^2 \rightarrow c = 10$

21) The answer is 240.

Th ratio of boy to girls is $2:3$. Therefore, there are 2 boys out of 5 students. To find the answer, first divide the total number of students by 5, then multiply the result by 2.
$600 \div 5 = 120 \Rightarrow 120 \times 2 = 240$

22) Choice C is correct

Use percent formula: part $= \frac{percent}{100} \times$ whole
$25 = \frac{percent}{100} \times 20 \Rightarrow 25 = \frac{percent \times 20}{100} \Rightarrow 25 = \frac{percent \times 2}{10}$, multiply both sides by 10.
$250 = percent \times 2$, divide both sides by 2. $125 = percent$

23) The answer is 130.

The perimeter of the trapezoid is 64.

Therefore, the missing side (height) is $= 64 - 18 - 12 - 14 = 10$

Area of a trapezoid: $A = \frac{1}{2} h (b_1 + b_2) = \frac{1}{2}(10)(12 + 14) = 130$

24) Choice C is correct

Let x be the number. Write the equation and solve for x.

$\frac{2}{3} \times 18 = \frac{2}{5}x \Rightarrow \frac{2 \times 18}{3} = \frac{2x}{5}$, use cross multiplication to solve for x.

$5 \times 36 = 2x \times 3 \Rightarrow 180 = 6x \Rightarrow x = 30$

25) Choice B is correct

To find the discount, multiply the number by $(100\% - rate\ of\ discount)$.

Therefore, for the first discount we get: $(D)(100\% - 20\%) = (D)(0.80) = 0.80\ D$

For increase of 10%: $(0.80\ D)(100\% + 10\%) = (0.80D)(1.10) = 0.88\ D = 88\%\ of\ D$

26) Choice B is correct

Use the formula of areas of circles.

$Area = \pi r^2 \Rightarrow 64\pi = \pi r^2 \Rightarrow 64 = r^2 \Rightarrow r = 8$

Radius of the circle is 8. Now, use the circumference formula:

Circumference$= 2\pi r = 2\pi(8) = 16\pi$

27) Choice B is correct

Use the formula for Percent of Change. $\frac{New\ Value - Old\ Value}{Old\ Value} \times 100\ \%$

$\frac{28-40}{40} \times 100\% = -30\%$ (negative sign here means that the new price is less than old price).

28) Choice A is correct

Let x be the number of years. Therefore, \$2,000 per year equals $2,000x$. starting from \$24,000 annual salary means you should add that amount to $2,000x$. Income more than that is: $I > 2,000x + 24,000$

29) Choice C is correct

The question is this: 1.75 is what percent of 1.25? Use percent formula:

$part = \dfrac{percent}{100} \times whole \Rightarrow 1.75 = \dfrac{percent}{100} \times 1.25 \Rightarrow 1.75 = \dfrac{percent \times 1.25}{100} \Rightarrow$

$175 = percent \times 1.25 \Rightarrow percent = \dfrac{175}{1.25} = 140$

30) Choice B is correct

Use the information provided in the question to draw the shape.
Use Pythagorean Theorem: $a^2 + b^2 = c^2$
$40^2 + 30^2 = c^2 \Rightarrow 1600 + 900 = c^2 \Rightarrow 2500 = c^2 \Rightarrow c = 50$

40 miles

30 miles

31) Choice D is correct

Some of prime numbers are: $2, 3, 5, 7, 11, 13$

Find the product of two consecutive prime numbers: $2 \times 3 = 6$ (not in the options) $3 \times 5 = 15$ (bingo!), $5 \times 7 = 35$ (not in the options)

32) Choice B is correct

The question is this: 529.72 is what percent of 646? Use percent formula:

$part = \dfrac{percent}{100} \times whole \rightarrow 529.72 = \dfrac{percent}{100} \times 646 \rightarrow 529.72$

$= \dfrac{percent \times 646}{100} \rightarrow 52,972 = percent \times 646 \rightarrow percent = \dfrac{52,972}{646} = 82$

529.72 is 82% of 646. Therefore, the discount is: $100\% - 82\% = 18\%$

33) Choice B is correct

If the score of Mia was 40, therefore the score of Ava is 20. Since, the score of Emma was half as that of Ava, therefore, the score of Emma is 10.

34) Choice D is correct

If 17 balls are removed from the bag at random, there will be one ball in the bag. The probability of choosing a brown ball is 1 out of 18. Therefore, the probability of not choosing a brown ball is 17 out of 18 and the probability of having not a brown ball after removing 17 balls is the same.

35) Choice B is correct

Let x be the smallest number. Then, these are the numbers: x, $x + 1$, $x + 2$, $x + 3$, $x + 4$

average $= \frac{\text{sum of terms}}{\text{number of terms}} \Rightarrow 38 = \frac{x+(x+1)+(x+2)+(x+3)+(x+4)}{5} \Rightarrow 38 = \frac{5x+10}{5} \Rightarrow$

$190 = 5x + 10 \Rightarrow 180 = 5x \Rightarrow x = 36$

36) Choice D is correct

The area of the floor is: $8 \ cm \times 24 \ cm = 192 \ cm^2$. The number of tiles needed $= 192 \div 8 = 24$

37) Choice C is correct

The weight of 12.2 meters of this rope is: $12.2 \times 600 \ g = 7320 \ g$
$1 \ kg = 1000 \ g$, therefore, $7320 \ g \div 1000 = 7.32 \ kg$

38) Choice C is correct

4% of the volume of the solution is alcohol. Let x be the volume of the solution.
Then: $4\% \ of \ x = 32 \ ml \Rightarrow 0.04 \ x = 32 \Rightarrow x = 32 \div 0.04 = 800$

39) Choice B is correct

average $= \frac{\text{sum of terms}}{\text{number of terms}}$. The sum of the weight of all girls is: $23 \times 60 = 1,380 \ kg$, The sum of the weight of all boys is: $32 \times 62 = 1984 \ kg$. The sum of the weight of all students is: $1,380 + 1,984 = 3,364 \ kg$. $average = \frac{3,364}{55} = 61.16$

40) Choice D is correct

Let x be the original price. If the price of a laptop is decreased by 20% to $360, then:
$80\% \ of \ x = 360 \Rightarrow 0.80x = 360 \Rightarrow x = 360 \div 0.80 = 450$

41) Choice B is correct

Write the numbers in order: $3, 5, 8, 10, 13, 15, 19$

Since we have 7 numbers (7 is odd), then the median is the number in the middle, which is 10.

42) The answer is 678.24.

Surface Area of a cylinder $= 2\pi r(r + h)$, The radius of the cylinder is 6 inches and its height is 12 inches. π is about 3.14. Then: Surface Area of a cylinder $= 2(\pi)(6)(6 + 12) = 216\pi = 678.24$

43) The answer is 12.

$$average = \frac{sum\ of\ terms}{number\ of\ terms} \Rightarrow 15 = \frac{13 + 15 + 20 + x}{4} \Rightarrow 60 = 48 + x \Rightarrow x = 12$$

44) Choice C is correct

Let x be the original price. If the price of the sofa is decreased by 25% to $\$420$, then: $75\%\ of\ x = 420 \Rightarrow 0.75x = 420 \Rightarrow x = 420 \div 0.75 = 560$

45) Choice D and E are correct

(If you selected 3 choices and 2 of them are correct, then you get one point. If you answered 2 or 3 choices and one of them is correct, you receive one point. If you selected more than 3 choices, you won't get any point for this question.) The equation of a line is in the form of $y = mx + b$, where m is the slope of the line and b is the $y - intercept$ of the line. Two points $(1, 2)$ and $(-1, 6)$ are on line A. Therefore, the slope of the line A is: $slope\ of\ line\ A = \frac{y_2 - y_1}{x_2 - x_1} = \frac{6-2}{-1-1} = \frac{4}{-2} = -2$

The slope of line A is -2. Thus, the formula of the line A is: $y = mx + b = -2x + b$, choose a point and plug in the values of x and y in the equation to solve for b. Let's choose point $(1, 2)$. Then: $y = -2x + b \rightarrow 2 = -2(1) + b \rightarrow b = 2 + 2 = 4$. The equation of line A is: $y = -2x + 4$

Now, let's review the choices provided:

A. $(-1, 2) \rightarrow y = -2x + 4 \rightarrow 2 = -2(-1) + 4 = 6 \rightarrow$ This is not true.

B. $(5,7) \rightarrow y = -2x + 4 \rightarrow 7 = -2(5) + 4 = -6 \rightarrow$ This is not true.

C. $(3,4) \rightarrow y = -2x + 4 \rightarrow 4 = -2(3) + 4 = -2 \rightarrow$ This is not true.

D. $(3,-2) \rightarrow y = -2x + 4 \rightarrow -2 = -2(3) + 4 = -2 \rightarrow$ This is true!

E. $(6,-8) \rightarrow y = -2x + 4 \rightarrow -8 = -2(6) + 4 = -8 \rightarrow$ This is true!

46) Choice C is correct

Use simple interest formula: $I = prt$ ($I = interest, p = principal, r = rate, t = time$) $I = (9,000)(0.045)(5) = 2,025$

$I = (9,000)(0.045)(5) = 2,025$

GED Mathematical Reasoning Practice Test 2
Answers and Explanations

1) Choice D is correct

$3x - 5 = 8.5 \rightarrow 3x = 8.5 + 5 = 13.5 \rightarrow x = \frac{13.5}{3} = 4.5$

Then; $6x + 3 = 6(4.5) + 3 = 27 + 3 = 30$

2) Choice D is correct

First draw an isosceles triangle. Remember that
two sides of the triangle are equal.

Let put a for the legs. Then:

$a = 8 \Rightarrow$ area of the triangle is $= \frac{1}{2}(8 \times 8) = \frac{64}{2} = 32 \; cm^2$

Isosceles right triangle

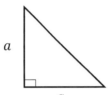

3) Choice D is correct

To find the discount, multiply the number by $(100\% - rate\ of\ discount)$.
Therefore, for the first discount we get: $(600)\ (100\% - 25\%) = (600)\ (0.75)$
For the next 15% discount: $(600)(0.75)(0.85)$.

4) Choice A is correct

Plug in each pair of numbers in the equation: $3x + 5y = 11$

A. $(2,1)$: $3\ (2) + 5\ (1) = 11$

B. $(-1,2)$: $3\ (-1) + 5\ (2) = 7$

C. $(-2,2)$: $3\ (-2) + 5\ (2) = 4$

D. $(2,2)$: $3\ (2) + 5\ (2) = 16$

Choice A is correct.

5) The answer is -3.

Use PEMDAS (order of operation): $-15 + 6 \times (-5) - [4 + 22 \times (-4)] \div 2 =$
$-15 - 30 - [4 - 88] \div 2 = -45 - [-84] \div 2 = -45 + 84 \div 2 = -45 + 42 = -3$

6) Choice A is correct

Let x be the smallest number. Then, these are the numbers: x, $x + 1$, $x + 2$, $x + 3$, $x + 4$

average $= \frac{\text{sum of terms}}{\text{number of terms}} \Rightarrow 40 = \frac{x+(x+1)+(x+2)+(x+3)+(x+4)}{5} \Rightarrow 40 = \frac{5x+10}{5} \Rightarrow 200 = 5x + 10 \Rightarrow 190 = 5x \Rightarrow x = 38$

7) Choice C is correct

The area of the floor is: $7 \, cm \times 24 \, cm = 168 \, cm^2$, The number of tiles needed $= 168 \div 8 = 21$

8) Choice C is correct

The weight of 15.2 meters of this rope is: $15.2 \times 600 \, g = 9{,}120 \, g$, $1 \, kg = 1{,}000 \, g$, therefore, $7{,}320 \, g \div 1000 = 9.12 \, kg$

9) Choice B is correct

6% of the volume of the solution is alcohol. Let x be the volume of the solution.

Then: $6\% \, of \, x = 24 \, ml \Rightarrow 0.06 \, x = 24 \Rightarrow x = 24 \div 0.06 = 400$

10) Choice B is correct

average $= \frac{\text{sum of terms}}{\text{number of terms}}$

The sum of the weight of all girls is: $18 \times 60 = 1080 \, kg$, The sum of the weight of all boys is: $32 \times 62 = 1984 \, kg$, The sum of the weight of all students is: $1080 + 1984 = 3064 \, kg$

average $= \frac{3064}{50} = 61.28$

11) Choice C is correct

Let x be the original price. If the price of a laptop is decreased by 10% to \$360, then:

$90\% \, of \, x = 360 \Rightarrow 0.90x = 360 \Rightarrow x = 360 \div 0.90 = 400$

12) Choice B is correct

Write the numbers in order: $4, 5, 8, 9, 13, 15, 18$
Since we have 7 numbers (7 is odd), then the median is the number in the middle, which is 9.

13) The answer is 1,205.76

Surface Area of a cylinder $= 2\pi r \, (r + h)$,
The radius of the cylinder is 8 inches and its height is 12 inches. π is 3.14. Then:
Surface Area of a cylinder $= 2 \, (3.14) \, (8) \, (8 + 16) = 1205.76$

14) Choice A is correct

Let x be the number of years. Therefore, $\$2,000 \, per \, year$ equals $2000x$. starting from $\$27,000$ annual salary means you should add that amount to $2,000x$.
Income more than that is: $I > 2000x + 27000$

15) The answer is 5

Solving Systems of Equations by Elimination
$\begin{array}{r} 3x - 4y = -20 \\ -x + 2y = 10 \end{array}$ $\Rightarrow$ Multiply the second equation by 3, then add it to the first equation.
$\begin{array}{r} 3x - 4y = -20 \\ 3(-x + 2y = 10) \end{array} \Rightarrow \begin{array}{r} 3x - 4y = -20 \\ -3x + 6y = 30) \end{array} \Rightarrow 2y = 10 \Rightarrow y = 5$

16) Choice B is correct

The diagonal of the square is 6 meters. Let x be the side.
Use Pythagorean Theorem: $a^2 + b^2 = c^2$
$x^2 + x^2 = 6^2 \Rightarrow 2x^2 = 6^2 \Rightarrow 2x^2 = 36 \Rightarrow x^2 = 18 \Rightarrow x = \sqrt{18}$
The area of the square is: $\sqrt{18} \times \sqrt{18} = 18 \; m^2$

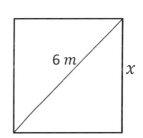

17) Choice D is correct

If the length of the box is 24, then the width of the box is one third of it, 8, and the height of the box is 4 (half of the width). The volume of the box is: $V = lwh = (24)(8)(4) = 768$

18) Choice D is correct

Write the equation and solve for B: $0.60A = 0.20B$, divide both sides by 0.20, then: $\frac{0.60}{0.20}A = B$, therefore: $B = 3A$, and B is 3 times of A or it's 300% of A.

19) The answer is 108.

To find the number of possible outfit combinations, multiply number of options for each factor:
$6 \times 3 \times 6 = 108$

20) Choice C is correct

Use simple interest formula: $I = prt$ ($I = interest$, $p = principal$, $r = rate$, $t = time$)
$I = (8,000)(0.025)(5) = 1,000$

21) The answer is 7,776

$6^5 = 6 \times 6 \times 6 \times 6 \times 6 = 7,776$

22) Choice B is correct

Use percent formula: $part = \frac{percent}{100} \times whole$. $15 = \frac{percent}{100} \times 20 \Rightarrow 15 = \frac{percent \times 20}{100} \Rightarrow 15 = \frac{percent \times 2}{10}$, multiply both sides by 10. $150 = percent \times 2$, divide both sides by 2. $75 = percent$

23) The answer is 78.

The perimeter of the trapezoid is 50. Therefore, the missing side (height) is $= 50 - 18 - 12 - 14 = 6$, Area of a trapezoid: $A = \frac{1}{2} h (b_1 + b_2) = \frac{1}{2} (6)(12 + 14) = 78$

24) Choice B is correct

Add the first 5 numbers. $40 + 45 + 50 + 35 + 55 = 225$

To find the distance traveled in the next 5 hours, multiply the average by number of hours.

Distance = Average × Rate = $45 \times 5 = 225$, Add both numbers. $225 + 225 = 450$

25) Choice B is correct

Use distance formula: $Distance = Rate \times time \Rightarrow 420 = 60 \times T$, divide both sides by 60. $\frac{420}{60} = T \Rightarrow T = 7 \ hours$

26) Choice D is correct.

Plug in each pair of numbers in the equation. The answer should be 20.

A. $(2, 1): 4(2) + 6(1) = 14 \rightarrow$No!

B. $(-1, 3): 4(-1) + 6(2) = 8 \rightarrow$No!

C. $(-2, 2): 4(-2) + 6(2) = 4 \rightarrow$No!

D. $(2, 2): 4(2) + 6(2) = 20 \rightarrow$Yes!

27) Choice C is correct

Let x be the number. Write the equation and solve for x.

$\frac{2}{3} \times 15 = \frac{2}{5}x \Rightarrow \frac{2 \times 15}{3} = \frac{2x}{5}$, use cross multiplication to solve for x.

$5 \times 30 = 2x \times 3 \Rightarrow 150 = 6x \Rightarrow x = 25$

28) Choice C is correct

To find the discount, multiply the number by $(100\% - rate \ of \ discount)$.

Therefore, for the first discount we get: $(D)(100\% - 20\%) = (D)(0.80) = 0.80 \ D$

For increase of 15%:

$(0.80D)(100\% + 15\%) = (0.80 \ D)(1.15) = 0.92 \ D = 92\% \ of \ D$

29) Choice B is correct

Use the formula for Percent of Change: $\frac{New \ Value - Old \ Value}{Old \ Value} \times 100\%$

$\frac{28 - 45}{45} \times 100\% = -37.7\%$ (negative sign here means that the new price is less than old price).

30) Choices D and E are correct

(If you selected 3 choices and 2 of them are correct, then you get one point. If you answered 2 or 3 choices and one of them is correct, you receive one point. If you selected more than 3 choices, you won't get any point for this question.) Some of prime numbers are: $2, 3, 5, 7, 11, 13$. Find the product of two consecutive prime numbers: $2 \times 3 = 6$ (not in the options), $3 \times 5 = 15$ (bingo!), $5 \times 7 = 35$ (yes!) ,$7 \times 11 = 77$ (not in the options). Choices D and E are correct.

31) The answer is 160.

Th ratio of boy to girls is $2 : 3$. Therefore, there are 2 boys out of 5 students. To find the answer, first divide the total number of students by 5, then multiply the result by 2.
$400 \div 5 = 80 \Rightarrow 80 \times 2 = 160$

32) Choice B is correct

$$percent = \frac{537.50}{625} = 0.86 = 86\%$$
537.50 is 86% of 625. Therefore, the discount is: $100\% - 86\% = 14\%$

33) Choice B is correct

If the score of Mia was 60, therefore the score of Ava is 30. Since the score of Emma was half as that of Ava, therefore, the score of Emma is 15.

34) Choice D is correct

If 20 balls are removed from the bag at random, there will be one ball in the bag. The probability of choosing a white ball is 1 out of 21. Therefore, the probability of not choosing a white ball is 20 out of 21 and the probability of having not a white ball after removing 20 balls is the same.

35) Choice D is correct

$8 \times 10 = \$80$, Petrol use: $10 \times 2 = 20$ liters, Petrol cost: $20 \times \$1 = \$20$
Money earned: $\$80 - \$20 = \$60$

36) The answer is 52.

$$\text{average} = \frac{\text{sum of terms}}{\text{number of terms}} \Rightarrow 25 = \frac{13+15+20+x}{4} \Rightarrow 100 = 48 + x \Rightarrow x = 52$$

37) Choice C is correct

Let x be the original price. If the price of the sofa is decreased by 15% to $476, then: 85% $of \; x = 476 \Rightarrow 0.85x = 476 \Rightarrow x = 476 \div 0.85 = 560$

38) Choice C is correct

Let x be the number. Write the equation and solve for x. $(28 - x) \div x = 3$
Multiply both sides by x. $(28 - x) = 3x$, then add x both sides. $28 = 4x$, now divide both sides by 4. $x = 7$

39) Choice C is correct

The sum of supplement angles is 180. Let x be that angle.
Therefore, $x + 4x = 180$
$5x = 180$, divide both sides by 5: $x = 36$

40) Choice C is correct

The average speed of john is: $150 \div 6 = 25 \; km$. The average speed of Alice is: $160 \div 4 = 40 \; km$. Write the ratio and simplify. $25:40 \Rightarrow 5:8$

41) Choice C is correct

Use Pythagorean Theorem: $a^2 + b^2 = c^2$
$5^2 + 12^2 = c^2 \Rightarrow 25 + 144 = c^2 \Rightarrow 169 = c^2 \Rightarrow c = 13$

42) Choice A is correct

The percent of girls take drawing class is: $75\% \times \frac{1}{3} = 25\%$

43) Choices A and B are correct

(If you selected 3 choices and 2 of them are correct, then you get one point. If you answered 2 or 3 choices and one of them is correct, you receive one point. If you selected more than 3 choices, you won't get any point for this question.)

Area of the circle is less than $14\,\pi$. Use the formula of areas of circles.

$Area = \pi r^2 \Rightarrow 49\,\pi > \pi r^2 \Rightarrow 49 > r^2 \Rightarrow r < 7$

Radius of the circle is less than 7. Let's put 7 for the radius. Now, use the circumference formula: $Circumference = 2\pi r = 2\pi\,(7) = 14\pi$. Since the radius of the circle is less than 7. Then, the circumference of the circle must be less than 14π. Only choices A and B are less than 14π.

44) Choice D and E are correct

Simplify the inequality: $2y + 6 < 30 \rightarrow 2y < 30 - 6 \rightarrow 2y < 24 \rightarrow y < 12$. Only choices D (8) and E (−12) are less than 12.

45) Choice C is correct

The question is this: 185.00 is what percent of 125.00? Use percent formula: $\frac{185}{125} = 1.48$ or 148%

46) Choice B is correct

Use the information provided in the question to draw the shape.
Use Pythagorean Theorem: $a^2 + b^2 = c^2$
$80^2 + 150^2 = c^2 \Rightarrow 6{,}400 + 22{,}500 = c^2 \Rightarrow 28{,}900 = c^2 \Rightarrow c = 170$

80 *miles*

150 *miles*

Receive the PDF version of this book or get another FREE book!

Thank you for using our Book!

Do you LOVE this book?

Then, you can get the PDF version of this book or another book absolutely FREE!

Please email us at:

info@EffortlessMath.com

for details.

Author's Final Note

I hope you enjoyed reading this book. You've made it through the book! Great job!

First of all, thank you for purchasing this study guide. I know you could have picked any number of books to help you prepare for your GED Math test, but you picked this book and for that I am extremely grateful.

It took me years to write this study guide for the GED Math because I wanted to prepare a comprehensive GED Math study guide to help test takers make the most effective use of their valuable time while preparing for the test.

After teaching and tutoring math courses for over a decade, I've gathered my personal notes and lessons to develop this study guide. It is my greatest hope that the lessons in this book could help you prepare for your test successfully.

If you have any questions, please contact me at reza@effortlessmath.com and I will be glad to assist. Your feedback will help me to greatly improve the quality of my books in the future and make this book even better. Furthermore, I expect that I have made a few minor errors somewhere in this study guide. If you think this to be the case, please let me know so I can fix the issue as soon as possible.

If you enjoyed this book and found some benefit in reading this, I'd like to hear from you and hope that you could take a quick minute to post a review on the book's Amazon page. To leave your valuable feedback, please visit: rb.gy/ycnwgk

Or scan this QR code.

I personally go over every single review, to make sure my books really are reaching out and helping students and test takers. Please help me help GED Math test takers, by leaving a review!

I wish you all the best in your future success!

Reza Nazari

Math teacher and author

Made in the USA
Monee, IL
12 April 2023

31737470R00120